ROD WALES

FURNITURE
PROJECTS

D1379851

Guild of Master Craftsman Publications

Guild of Master Craftsman Publications

First Published 1991 by
Guild of Master Craftsman Publications Ltd,
Castle Place, 166 High Street,
Lewes, East Sussex BN7 1XU

© **Rod Wales 1991**

ISBN 0 946819 25 4

Designed by Fineline Studios

Printed and bound in Great Britain by Bell & Bain Ltd., Glasgow.

CONTENTS

Introduction   5

PROJECTS

Author's Note   17

Blanket Chest   18

Corner Cabinet   28

Coatstand   36

Mirror   42

Computer Desk and Drawer Unit   48

Informal Form   56

Wave Bench   60

Nest of Tables   64

Garden Seat   70

Pair of Tables   76

CD Storage Shelving   82

Alcove Shelving   90

Low Table   100

Office Desk and Drawers   108

Office Meeting Table   116

To Ali, the sine qua non

Acknowledgements

Furniture designed by Wales and Wales
and made in their workshop by
Simon Crowe
Richard Handy
Kim Sheard
Paul Stratton
Wycliffe Stutchbury
Rod Wales

Photography by
Derek Gardiner
Michael Hemsley
Phil Grey
Karen Norquay
Paul Noble
Derry Robinson

INTRODUCTION

It has been roughly fifteen years since I began learning how to make anything. That it was wood I made it with was unpremeditated, circumstantial, and yet maybe not altogether an accident. To some extent, choices are determined by what is accessible, but I'm sure that intuition played a part in making me a woodworker: that and, I suspect, a fair degree of indirect cultural conditioning.

Brought up in the backwoods of suburban London, relatively leafy though they may be, I was unlikely to encounter the spirit of the trees: the Green Man meant nothing more than a somewhat decrepit boozer hard by the municipal baths. Nevertheless, being English, knowing a bit of history and gradually becoming aware of the mysterious, bewildering variety of wood around the place, I began to sense, in a boyish and disengaged way, the significance of the material. Sailing ships, longbows, cricket bats; that sort of thing. Definitely not furniture.

Jumping ahead a decade or so, however, on a visit to the Wallace Collection in London I was distracted from the paintings by the extraordinary French eighteenth-century furniture – I seem to remember the 'Laughing Cavalier' grimacing knowingly as I crawled around checking out the marquetry. My opinion of the French ébénistes has changed in the intervening years, but at the time it was not merely the quality of workmanship, but the intensity of feeling required to produce such work that initially attracted me. Curious really, as at the time I had not the faintest notion of how to make anything at all; my abiding memory of school woodwork was (still is) of not being able to get two or three pieces of mangled softwood to convince anyone of their being a teapot stand. Making things had always been somebody else's business: suddenly I wanted it to be mine.

Innocent of any technical background as I was, the ensuing education proved to be a fairly bumpy ride and not without its moments of despair, but now I had discovered a personal need to make things and it soon began to seem worth it, despite the slog.

Wood is an extraordinarily rich and diverse substance, difficult and unforgiving if abused, demanding of considerable and precise understanding. Before it can be worked with, it has to be worked at, and this requires discipline, a fair bit of time and, ideally, one or more good teachers. It is an arduous process – but then learning anything thoroughly and purposefully occurs as a series of stages, even as a leisure activity. (No-one learns to ride a bike by entering the Tour de France, but to wobble off on a wheel and a prayer and make the circuit of the playground without causing serious injury is to enter the next stage wearing the yellow jersey.) I wasn't thinking deeply about making at this stage – that possibility had yet to dawn on me – it was a matter of getting my head down and my hands dirty. Trying to get them – and the tools – to do what they were told was enough to be going on with.

Rycotewood College provided an excellent basis for all this, and towards the end of my time there Alan Peters saw my work, gently pointed out just how far I had yet to go, but encouraged me to take it further. A year as a college technician followed, a time that certainly benefited me more than the establishment in question. By now the first stirrings of a design consciousness were beginning to ally themselves to this messy business of making things, and I was given the opportunity to develop this and generally raise my game at the School for Craftsmen in Wood at Parnham. Among very many other things, this course was a preparation for self-employment as a designer-maker. It was a tremendously rich educational mixture and, while it was certainly exciting and immediately productive, in some respects it was so rich as to need some time to digest. Absorbing and developing a personal view of design philosophies as diverse as those of, for instance, Wendell Castle and James Krenov, to say nothing of John Makepeace himself, is not the work of a moment. Eventually, primed and loaded, if somewhat uncertainly aimed, I set up shop early in 1981.

The workshop was initially shared with two other craftsmen. Though much has changed in the intervening years, our business still remains in the same place and the work shown in colour following this section gives an idea of some of the developments during that time.

For the first five or six years the work was comprised of little else but modest domestic commissions. More recently, rising costs, expansion of the workshop and a desire to develop and address our abilities to a broader market have led us further into what might be described as the commercial mainstream. This has led to increasing collaboration with architects and other designers, who have generally been happy to recognise and employ our design skills along with our capacity for making things. (You notice the language has changed: 'I' has become 'we', not only in deference to my wife Alison, with whom I now design everything, but also to acknowledge that the workshop is itself a shared enterprise.)

This book is not the place for a treatise on design, but within these projects I have attempted to convey some idea of the factors that shaped the thinking behind them. The purpose of this introduction is both to provide a broader perspective from which to view the projects, and to describe something of my attitude to design. Without wishing to sound on the one hand pompous or simplistic on the other, I believe it is possible to consider the subject seriously without drowning in theory.

Although the projects in this book are directed in a very practical way at woodworkers, I hope they will also prompt some consideration of design beyond the immediate constructional issues, as I believe it is vital to examine our motives for working in any particular way. Really good work goes beyond immediate practical or material concerns. This complex of physical and psychological factors partially derives from the maker's understanding of *why* an object is to be made in a particular way, and the effect that will have on the finished piece. The process of making, whether artful, crafty or anything else, is a mediation, a secondary action. A preliminary is inevitable, which is design. This is an emotive subject to say the least, but as makers, responsible for both invention and construction, it is important (that is, it may well be productive) to bite the bullet and think about what the implications of this tricky little word 'design' are, and how they actually affect the work we do.

Constructional practice and technical feasibility will always contribute to the way an object looks and works – and can do so very positively – but it seems to be a special curse of woodworkers to believe that 'design' consists of figuring out the joint (especially if it's a dovetail!): this view is both blinkered and shortsighted, and leads to narrow-mindedness. Another problem common among the dusty fraternity is caused by the very seductiveness of the material, or more properly range of materials – and unfortunately it is only too easy to make a pig's ear out of a silk purse. Sensitivity to the material and its particular potential is crucial, but pretty grain does not absolve a multitude of sins (of omission or commission), and actually flaunting it can often amount to little more than careless or, worse, cynical sentiment.

Good design is never effortless, however much it may appear so; it takes time to arrive at a personal language and then use the vocabulary successfully. Neither does good design occur in a vacuum: it consists of a series of decisions based on objective information and a knowledge of the constraints within a particular situation. 'Inspiration' has more to do with the excitement and tension generated by these constraints than with great ideas falling like manna from heaven.

I believe it is impossible to offer a neat one-liner as a genuinely useful prescription for good design (despite a sneaking regard for the venerable 'commodity, firmness and delight'), because the factors continually shift and disperse, to be replaced by new requirements and questions, or else the definition becomes so general as to be practically meaningless. Nevertheless, I would wish to outline (no more) the principal factors that exercise me when designing, and which ultimately shape the work. None of these are original or exclusive, nor do they form a regular pattern. There is no checklist or rulebook. I am not making a map, but describing a route that has been followed, and sometimes erratically at that.

To return to the significance of construction and materials, I think it would be true to say that a major factor in getting most of us started is a straightforward delight in our materials. Despite the vast quantity of sentimental and extravagant claptrap which has been gushed forth on the subject of wood, it is undoubtedly wonderful stuff and I don't mind admitting that I love it. But, as with any love affair, a good deal of respect is required. Wood is as demanding as it is versatile, and a one-sided, obsessive interest in the pretty bits can quickly lead to abuse and boredom rather than celebration. Clarity of expression is an important overall objective, and is affected by the choice and treatment of the materials. One of the joys of working in wood is the enormous range of different timbers, which allows a flexible response from the designer. I am wary, however, of the temptations of highly figured timber, which, like other kinds of excess, can blunt the appetite and do terrible things to the digestion. It is certainly possible to achieve marvellous things with simple and commonplace ingredients.

Design is a constructive art, and structure and its means of construction derive largely from the nature of the material being used – these three factors together determine to a great extent the form of the object. Fortunately, the reality is less mechanical than this sounds. We are cussed folk, always wanting something different, something new, something personal. Individual interpretation – stretching and playing with the building blocks, intuitively or by strictly rational scientific means, or both, gives a huge variety of life and meaning to an otherwise arid concept.

This process of interpretation is also considerably affected by the personal chemistry between designer and client. This may appear most obviously in the relatively uncomplicated arrangement that usually occurs in a private commission, but can be equally evident when designing for production, in which case the customer multiplies to become a market. The product still has to find an individual end-user, though his or her aspirations and requirements for that product will have to be arrived at by other means than a cosy chat. Briefing, research and discussion extend beyond the purely practical requirements, and crucial to the outcome of the design process.

Closely related to this aspect of design is the response to context. This can be a useful and appropriate starting point, particularly in furniture design, which, after all, usually has to live in an environment that is, for better or worse, already built. A particular danger is too literal interpretation of context, which can result in design degenerating into mere styling, especially when responding to historical artefacts. The arbitrary and uncritical recycling of history actually denies tradition and makes it absurd, actively negating our heritage. I for one am more interested in the present than an illusory golden age – no matter what market research and my bank manager tell me – so I will try to be especially careful about quoting the past.

Although I cannot do justice to the subject of style – or indeed any of the issues related to the larger one of design itself – in so short a space, I would try to summarise it as ideally being a means of expressing personal values (not to be confused with self-expression), as distinct from the application of a superficial aesthetic. This need not confine us for ever after to one or even a few righteous paths: my enthusiasm for a Shaker cupboard, for example, doesn't diminish (though it may qualify) my esteem of Ettore Sottsass, and vice versa. What does worry me is the insensitive transfer of stylistic devices for their own sake, which tends to result in shallow decoration, bereft of any real meaning. A degree of honesty with yourself is necessary, to distinguish the useful and legitimate influence, which all designers have always enjoyed (and which will involve an understanding of and respect for the original intention), from casual theft.

I have regularly and deliberately sought a quality of simplicity in my work. By this I do not necessarily mean just a wholesome, unchallenging plainness (though that can be fine); understatement is part of it, combined with a reliance on composition, or the appropriate ordering of parts and details within the whole. I am not relentless in the pursuit of formal simplicity, which can so easily degenerate into sterility, but I am certainly attracted by minimal forms. That there is not much evidence of this unadorned purity in the work is largely because it is generally fatally compromised by domestic clutter, unless seen in extremely closely controlled and sympathetic

circumstances, i.e. a gallery. Most people cannot or do not wish to live in conditions which remotely resemble those of a gallery, or indeed those of an interior – untouched by human hand – as featured in a style magazine, and I must confess to feeling some sympathy there, despite occasional personal fantasies to the contrary.

Part of the problem with any obsessively rigorous and exclusive approach which does not concede anything to the ordinary realities of everyday life is that furniture, or indeed any designed object, becomes a master to be obeyed, to be bowed down to. This is not to say that we should design down to the lowest common denominator: I am interested in transforming rooms, not maintaining the status quo, but equally I am not in the business of making household gods. Perhaps we should exercise a little humility (which need not affect confidence) about what the effective limits of applied art are. Furniture can certainly approach the intensity of sculpture, but its purpose is different; its meaning is connected to its utility. While social responsibilities inevitably impinge on design to a greater extent than on fine art, aesthetic opportunity is not reduced by considerations of utility. It does however take nerve and commitment to fully explore the range of possibilities.

Now I work – and write – in a workshop, a place where the niceties of intellectual analysis can be very quickly displaced and forgotten. The work that follows is a product of that place; whether any of the above-mentioned qualities are apparent or otherwise is for you to judge. To gain a broader picture of what shapes my (our) attitude as a designer and maker, it is necessary to turn to work which provides a complementary context to the main event, but which is outside the scope of this book.

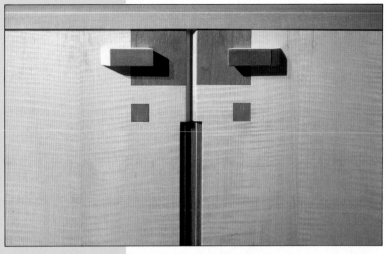

Handle detail. Inlay, chamfering and rebating on the closing edges of the doors to enliven an otherwise plain sycamore drinks cabinet.

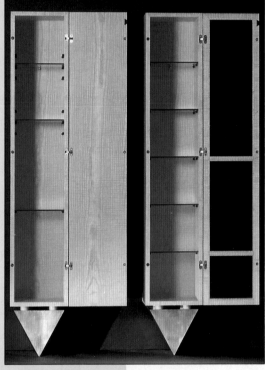

Wall hung/floor mounted cabinets: ash and pewter. A pair of cabinets to contain drink and a collection of pewter figures respectively. The major feature of the plinth reworked in the door pulls.

Bookcase with four doors and drawer: natural and fumed and limed oak.
Our first use of fumed and limed oak (in 1983) to create a contrast to the natural timber and to harmonise with the oak beams in a fifteenth-century farmhouse.

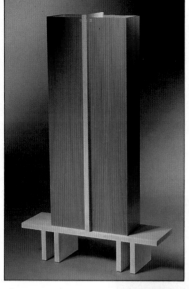

Sideboard: stained and natural Douglas fir, blued-steel details.
Materials, colour and construction in sympathy with those of the room.

Collectors cabinet: pearwood and limed ash.
The central section of a wall of shelving which carried through the line of the ash base, the cabinet was designed for a collection of stones, which are housed in the removable trays. An object that indicates the veneration with which the contents are regarded, it opens with a flourish. Initials of the customers and date of commission inlaid in boxwood.

Cabinet: fumed and limed oak, maple, stainless steel.
Commissioned as a 'conversation piece' for a sixteenth-century house, it contains guns and secrets. The form is a personal response to English oak furniture of the seventeenth century, and Japanese Edo period chests, but great pains were taken to avoid pastiche. The textural quality of the timber is emphasised by the use of contrasting smoothed and wire brushed panels, while the steel pinning derives from medieval door nailing.

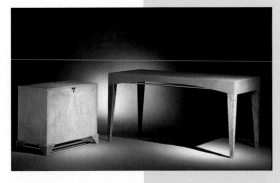

Writing table and filing cabinet: quilted maple, fumed and limed oak, stainless steel.
An emphatic contrast of materials, playing off the lustrous maple veneer against the tough, textured oak. The overall form is uncluttered, which allows the materials to work to maximum effect. The steel bracing rail on the table adds a little visual tension to the curve and provides another contrast to lift the whole piece.

Table: ash, brass.
A dining table for serious partying. The apparent likelihood of large men capering up there (a major feature of the brief) prompted special attention to the structure – a triangulated trestle with brass outriggers supporting a simple solid slab.

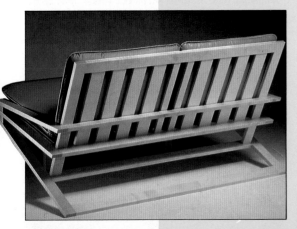

Double seat: sycamore.
A speculative piece made for an exhibition in 1982. It turns what is virtually a decorative arrangement of parts into a working structure.

Chairs: bleached and natural red oak.
Designed for a previously commissioned table. The backs are steam bent to provide good lumbar support. The customer requested each chair to be individually detailed, but remain part of a set.

Tripod table: ash, cherry, padauk.
An early attempt at a standard product, with laminated legs and lippings. The means of connecting the legs provides a satisfying joint detail (a happy example of process based design), but the top a little too reminiscent of eighteenth-century piecrusts perhaps?

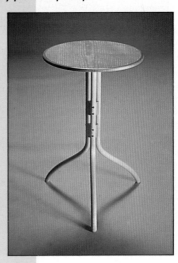

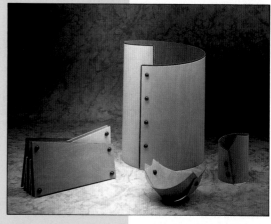

'Buttondown': plywood, nylon fixings.
A range of batch produced accessories (waste paper bin, desk tidy, letter rack and bowls). The flexible nature of the material (1.5 and .8mm 3-ply) originally suggested the design and was exploited in different ways in the various items.

Hall table: limed olive ash, bronze, stone.
A minimal form designed to contrast with – stand up to? – a very visually busy enamel screen. York stone slab copes with flower vases and relates to the floor material of the hall. The column contains three drawers. Scalloped edges provide unobtrusive finger grips.

Sine screen: plywood, ash, stainless steel.
A standard product, again using the qualities of thin plywood to create the form and decorative effect. The plywood is held in compression in its curves by the stainless steel rods passing through holes in the panels.

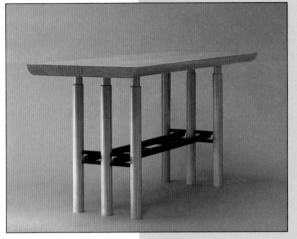

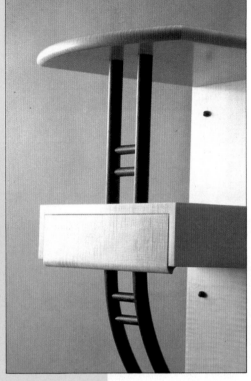

Television table: cherry and ebony.
The turned ebony rails stiffen the table legs and provide a
magazine rack while producing a contrast of scale and
material.

Detail of wall hung bedside cabinet: sycamore and
laminated wenge.

Three adjustable lecterns to fulfil similar functions, each
a development of the same structural idea, each destined
for a different environment. Their individuality is
achieved through considered detailing of the three main
elements: book rest, adjustable shaft, ground support, in
response to the building for which they were intended
and the specific requirements of the users.

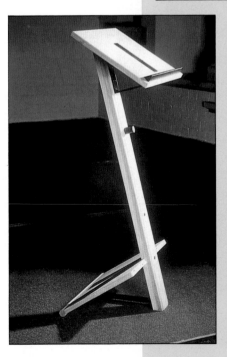

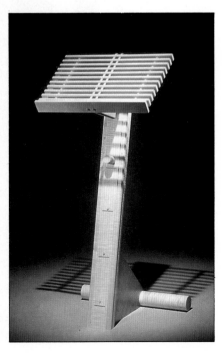

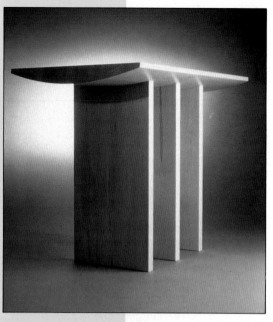

Chapel altar: maple and copper.
Part of the furniture (including lectern, credence table, president's chair and seating) for the chapel in St Mary's Hospital on the Isle of Wight. The curve underneath the top lightens and invigorates a very heavy slab of timber without diminishing its presence.

Reception desk: plywood and ash.
A low budget reception desk composed of interacting shaped planes of plywood and solid timber highlighted with coloured inlays and lippings.

Print box: sycamore.
One of six boxes commissioned to contain a set of prints by the artist Ana Maria Pecheco. The lid was designed as a base for her paintings, the turned detail as a location and a finger grip handle.

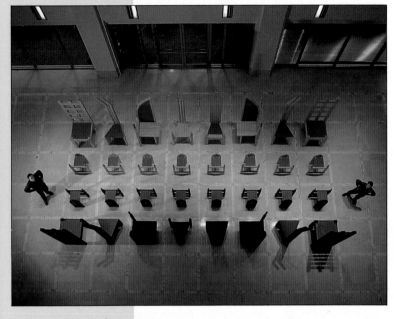

Chess chairs.
Commissioned through architects Skidmore, Owings and Merrill to occupy a central atrium in the Broadgate office development in the City of London. The ensemble makes a considerable visual and imaginative impact in a cool, ordered space. Each element interprets an archetypal chess figure within the form of a chair (a pawn as a stool, the king and queen as 2.7 metre thrones, etc.), loosely combining medieval military imagery and playful sculptural detail. Deeply grained shotblasted ash, steel and riven slate provide a strong textural and material contrast to the surrounding offices.

Standard bench for Canary Wharf.

Special bench for Canary Wharf.
We were asked to consider the design for outdoor public seating for Canary Wharf in Docklands as a result of the architect seeing our garden seat, which is one of the following projects. The standard bench was designed to convey the sense of a quality environment and reinforce a particular sense of place evoking London and its continuing tradition of urban squares and parks, as well as being a departure from the ubiquitous Edwardian garden seat. 250 units produced by a manufacturer will eventually grace the site. Twenty special benches were made in our workshop, an elaborated first cousin to the standard bench but site-specific to the square, where they are to be installed in pairs within granite faced niches.

Outdoor seat for Dun and Bradstreet headquarters in High Wycombe: unfinished Indonesian teak (from managed woodlands).
Three large benches facing the entrance to the new building. The bracing echoes elements of the canopy structure.

Bix bench: unfinished Indonesian teak.
A current standard product for outdoor public seating. Outstanding comfort and strength achieved by combining clarity of form and subtle detail.

AUTHOR'S NOTE

Furniture is about design and function. These two words often provoke enormous contention, but I use them here in their widest and least exclusive sense.

To briefly define the terms, I would suggest that design is an analytic and constructive activity while function covers a range of considerations, from the aesthetic to the utilitarian. Both design and function are affected by the problems of cost, and central to both is means of manufacture, the manner of the making, and in a very small way, that is what this book is about. It is, however, important to emphasise that this work is not intended to be generally prescriptive; even were such a thing desirable, the conditions that produced it are far too limited for that.

It may be helpful to realise that the pieces that comprise the substance of the book were made over the course of six or seven years, almost all of them for one customer and with the eventual intention of publishing them as these projects. These factors have had inevitable consequences on their design and technical content. Design does not take place in a vacuum. It tends to be push and pull, a call and response; the call as well as the response may very well be made by the designer, but the pattern remains – a creative solution in answer to a perceived need.

Now the person who pays the piper, not unreasonably, calls the tune, though this may leave considerable leeway as to the way it is played. Thus the projects here amount virtually to a family of pieces, not only by virtue (or otherwise) of their author, but if you like, by the circumstances of their birth. In each case I have written, to a greater or lesser extent, something of these conditions and what has prompted my response to them.

BLANKET CHEST

T

his commissioned piece is intended to function, and be responded to, in a variety of ways. It was to be sited in a generously proportioned entrance hall where it was meant to make an appropriate impression. The overall dimensions were fairly closely specified, as was the requirement for a drawer in the scheme. There was a possibility of the chest being used as a toy box for the two-year-old daughter of the household, though this was to be a relatively temporary function of a piece that would become a family heirloom.

BASICS OF DESIGN

Deciding upon a general arrangement and proportion I found acceptable was a lengthy process, I must at once

admit, involving scores if not hundreds of sketched ideas, half ideas and even half-baked ideas (just in case they turned into something usable), which were gradually worried into a coherent whole.

My intention was to integrate the various elements of the construction – the lid, carcase, drawer etc. – without allowing the visual unity to overwhelm and become homogeneous and bland. Thus details are echoed (but intentionally not repeated) in various parts of the design, and by simple means give the chest a degree of harmonious complexity.

CONSTRUCTION

The carcasing, lid frame and drawer front were in English cherry, the lid panels in sycamore and the feet, handles and details in African padauk.

Although they obviously overlap, to preserve clarity I shall break down the making sequence into three main parts and follow this order in the making: the carcase; the feet, drawer frame and drawer; the lid.

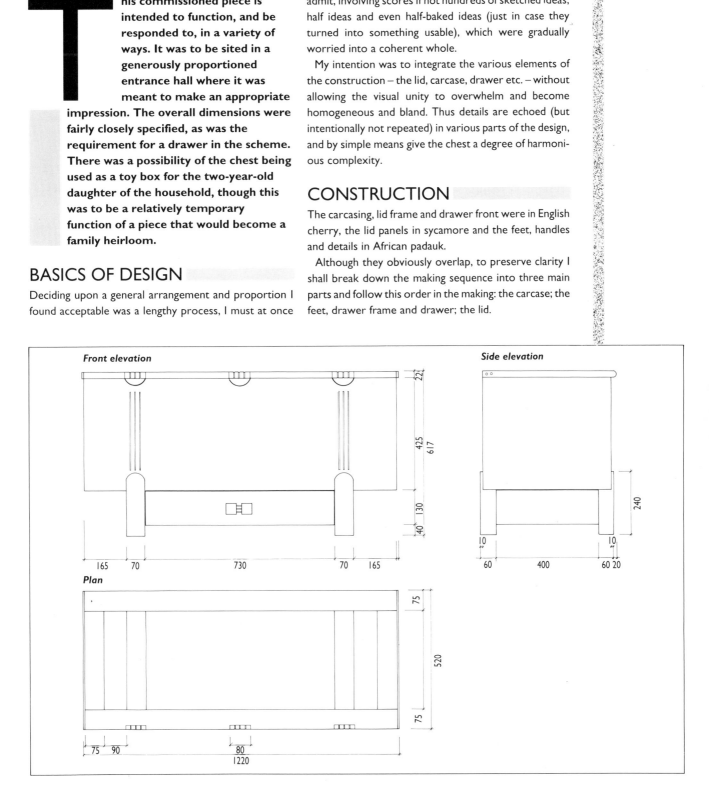

Front elevation

Side elevation

Plan

Router template for bridle joint

Feet bridled ready to fit

Side panels dovetailed and grooved

CARCASE

First the cherry was planked up, prepared to size and, having sorted and arranged the various boards to make up the most stable and attractive solid panels, the edges were shot by hand, biscuited and assembled.

The carcase can be jointed together in a variety of ways. Eventually I had to choose between two options: a mitre and tongue (or biscuit), or some form of dovetailing. I decided on the latter, despite the extra time involved and consequent squeeze on profit margins. (Since I made this piece, a number of dovetail jigs have appeared on the market which would accomplish this scale of dovetailing very well indeed. It would be foolish, however, to make the not inconsiderable investment in such a jig without a *continuous* need for it.)

I have an extremely accurate panel saw that would have enabled me to cut the mitre joint in probably a tenth of the time it took for the dovetails, but I felt the side of the chest needed some incident to offset the concentration of detail on the front. Dovetails seemed appropriate for this sort of piece – a chest is after all one of the earliest furniture types – and they are a reference to that whole tradition. They also add a feeling of robustness to the design, which I felt was becoming a touch too refined. I also enjoy it when one view of a piece of furniture (front elevation) reads differently to another (side elevation). Same voice: different story.

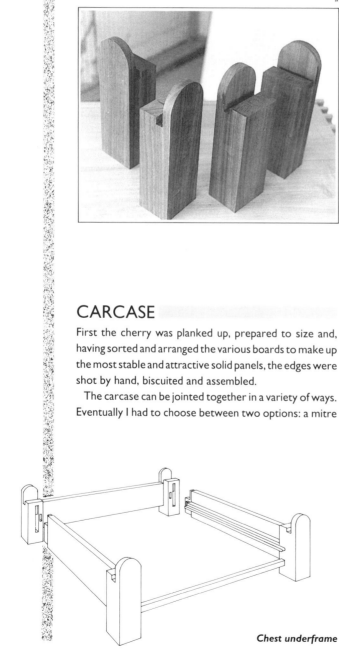

Chest underframe

In order to leave the front elevation visually unchanged, lap dovetails were used. The spacing of the dovetails was arranged symmetrically from the centre, the joints in pairs, decreasing in width towards the edges of the panel. This was done not so much to achieve greater strength by minimising the effects of timber movement, but to produce a visual tension. The lap was 6mm on a 22mm panel thickness. After marking out and sawing, the majority of the waste was removed from the tail sockets with a router. (I should mention here that I always cut the pins first, whatever form of dovetail I am cutting. I find this method gives greater room and more control in marking out.) Once the pins are cut and pared (in this case on the front and back panels), the tails are marked out from them. Some form of temporary support for the pin pieces will be needed as they will be liable to topple if not held.

Handle detail laminating

Gluing handle detail into recess

Side rail, drawer rail and guide arrangements

The bottom dovetail is designed to accommodate a groove to take the bottom panel of the box. In this case the panel was 10mm MDF rebated to fit a 6mm groove. The panel itself could of course be made from solid timber if desired – cedar or sycamore would be appropriate – but I had previously decided to line the chest and drawer, so a sheet material such as ply or MDF was better.

Before the carcase can be cleaned up and assembled, the joints for the feet must be cut. These take the form of a kind of long and short shouldered bridle joint, the long (front) side being shaped to a semicircle at the top. The short shoulder on the inside butts up to the underside of the bottom panel. As can be seen from the photographs

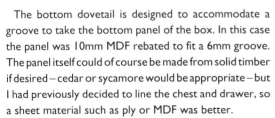

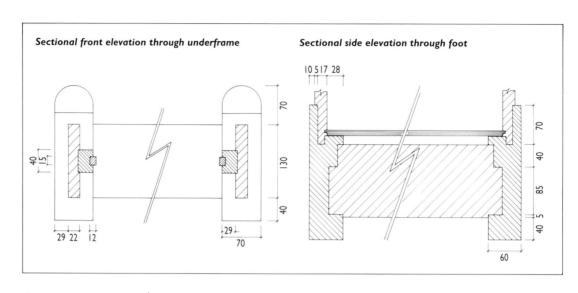

Sectional front elevation through underframe   Sectional side elevation through foot

Handle recess, fluting, bridle joint

I used a ply template, and a template follower on the router, to cut the recess on the outside of the panel.

For accuracy, cramp together the front and back panels and square across positions of the bridle joints on the bottom edges to line up the template, which will be slightly wider than the joint itself.

The exact size of the template will of course be determined by the relative sizes of the follower and cutter in use. The semicircle in the template can be cut with a tank cutter or expansion bit. The tangential lines on the front of the panel are squared up from the bottom edge, sawn and pared back. The short recess on the inside of the carcase panels can simply be routed and pared.

After preparing the feet to exact length, width and thickness (bandsaw and radial arm saw are the quickest means for this, I think) the bridle joint can be cut. To ensure identical accuracy on all four feet, I made a marking template for the front, which can be checked by fitting it into the routed recess. This also avoided the problem of a compass point on the face of the work. After so marking, the semicircle can be cut using a disc sander.

It is of course possible, logical even, to use the template to rout the curve. I did not do so because the face of the foot stands proud of the panel, and I was concerned not to have to sand out the inevitable tearing produced by routing end grain partly against the grain. Sanding like that would affect the accuracy of the joint.

After fitting, the face was given a 3mm chamfer, which was also taken round the bottom edges of the foot.

The next step was the handle recesses at the top edge of the front carcase panel. These could be cut quite easily by hand, but for consistency they were first sawn then routed from a template in the same way as the curved bridle recess.

The same template is used to make the negative side of the laminating former. The radius of the positive side is theoretically that of the negative less the thickness of the lay up. However, as I couldn't accurately predict how much the decorative thickness veneers would compress (and they varied slightly in thickness themselves), I used a slightly smaller radius and lined the former with thin cork. The veneer strips were cut with a generous allowance in the width and the former itself was thicker than the chest panel. Engineering tolerances are hardly applicable here, but the final lay up should be 5mm thick.

After completing the laminates, I lightly sanded the surface of the veneer to be fixed to the edge of the chest. As this was thoroughly impregnated with set adhesive already, I used an epoxy cement to glue the laminate on. Since most of the gluing surface was end grain, the laminate was also pinned at either end, the heads punched in, then one last veneer laminated on to hide the fixing. I might be accused of using 'belt and braces' here, but then again my trousers don't often fall down.

After trimming the handle detail the fluting can be marked out (centrally to the handle and foot), then routed in. Check the depth on scrap material and rout against a batten cramped to the panel. Be careful not to dwell at the beginning and end of the cuts as the consequent burning is awkward to remove without destroying the crispness of the line. It is worth grinding a scraper with the profile of the flute and making a special sanding block to deal with any problems in this respect.

The carcase is now ready for preliminary sanding – particularly inside, taking care not to affect the fit of the dovetails – then assembly.

DRAWER AND FRAME

The drawer frame consists of 2 side rails tenoned into the middle of the feet; the back rail, stub tenoned and positioned symmetrically to the drawer front, i.e. 1mm inside the carcase plane. The drawer rail is also stub tenoned.

Due to the position of the side rails it was necessary to provide a drawer guide and this also became the mount for the drawer runner itself. The guide was housed into the side rail and stub tenoned front and back. This tenon may seem superfluous (belt and braces again) but is designed to counteract the weight of the side-hung drawer, being its only support.

After fitting, the guide is itself housed to take the runner. The shoulder lengths of the side, back and drawer rails are critical, there being little or no tolerance if the feet are firmly joined to the carcase. These dimensions are best checked off the feet themselves, knocked home dry into the carcase. The drawer rail (between the two front feet) is set back to allow the drawer front to oversail. The

Drawer guide and runner

Drawer assembled prior to fitting

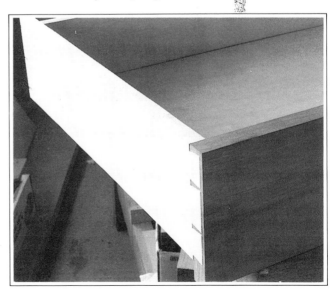

Paring and fitting drawer pull

Bead detail

drawer runner need only be screwed into its housing, lest subsequent easing be required when fitting the drawer.

Assembly of this underframe, including as it does the gluing of the feet to the carcase, will almost certainly require two pairs of hands and a glue with an open-assembly time of at least 20 minutes. A fast-setting glue is not desirable.

Have all the necessary sash cramps and cramping blocks available and set up before applying the glue. Once the glue is on, knock home the rails into the feet, then cramp the feet down on to the carcase to bring the bridle joint home. The rails can then be cramped. A certain amount of offsetting of cramps is inevitable as pressure (albeit only light pressure) is required in different directions simultaneously. When cleaning up squeeze-out, be particularly rigorous around the projecting curved bridle joint.

DRAWER

I would not usually dovetail an oversailing drawer front directly to the sides because of the difficulties of fitting the assembled drawer. But as this single drawer is side-hung a false front is unnecessary.

The drawer is constructed in the traditional manner, lap dovetailed at the front, through dovetailed at the back, with the bottom grooved in under the back. The sides and

Lid frame

back were of sycamore to match the panels in the lid; the bottom of 6mm ply rebated into the grooves. The component parts are first fitted to the opening in the usual way and the tail sockets cut in the front and back *fractionally* shallow. When assembled the sides are thus

Split turnings for handle

slightly proud and can then be planed back to the end of the pins.

With the runners removed the assembled drawer can be fitted to the opening, then the position of the groove to take the runner measured and routed. This groove need only be a maximum of 6mm deep but necessitates a slightly thicker drawer side than usual.

The pull is best marked out and cut prior to gluing up the drawer. The central recess is routed and the sloping sides pared down to it. The wedge section insert (inlaid with padauk) is then glued in. As the inlays are left proud, a cork-faced block is advisable when cramping.

LID

The lid is constructed in an absolutely traditional fashion, using haunched mortise and tenons for the end rails, the stub tenoned internal rails lining up with the feet and fluting on the carcase. The solid sycamore panels are rebated into grooves, and are set a millimetre down from the top face of the frame. After routing this rebate, the bead was worked with a scratch stock. With only three panels to do, I honestly think it was quicker than setting up the router, and anyway it saved buying a special cutter!

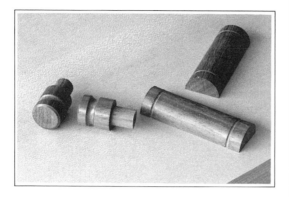

Spigots and split turnings for stays

The front of the frame oversails the front of the carcase to provide more of a purchase for the fingers. It is bull-nosed after the handles are fitted.

Once the lid has been assembled and cleaned up it can be hinged using 75mm solid drawn brass butts fixed in line with the internal rails. While the lid is hinged the position of the handles can be marked off from the recesses in the carcase. The slots for the handles can then be gauged, squared round and cut out. The inserts themselves are semi-cylindrical i.e. split turned, using paper in the glued joint between the two halves. After dividing the turning and cleaning up the face of the joint, the inserts are glued into their slots and the bull nose carefully planed and sanded down to them.

Finally I glued, screwed and plugged a 10mm strip of padauk to the short edges of the lid. This was done partly to provide a distinct line to the lid from the side, partly to cover the haunched mortise and tenon detail which didn't 'connect' coherently with the line of the dovetailing.

STAYS

The lid will need some form of stay. There are of course numerous proprietary examples available in brass, steel and/or plastic. They are on the whole awkward to fit, ugly, expensive and get in the way, so there isn't a lot to recommend them.

I decided to make a little feature of the fact that this chest was intended as a toy box and made a skipping rope stay. The 'handles' of the skipping rope were split turned then recessed for the rope and screwed to the underside of the lid, while two spigots were turned to take the loop at the opposite end. The loop in the rope was finished with whipping twine.

The chest was finished with Danish oil and waxed, and the bottom of both chest and drawer lined with felt.

Handle slot

Skipping rope stay

CUTTING LIST

Finished sizes

Front and back panels	2 x 1200 x 425 x 22	Cherry
Side panels	2 x 500 x 425 x 22	Cherry
Lid stiles	2 x 1200 x 75 x 22	Cherry
Lid rails	4 x 450 x 75 x 22	Cherry
Side rails	2 x 460 x 130 x 22	Cherry
Back rail	1 x 770 x 130 x 22	Cherry
Drawer front	1 x 730 x 130 x 22	Cherry
Drawer rail	1 x 770 x 20 x 20	Cherry
Drawer guides	2 x 430 x 40 x 29	Cherry
Drawer runners	2 x 420 x 15 x 12	Cherry
Drawer sides	2 x 400 x 110 x 13	Sycamore
Drawer back	1 x 730 x 90 x 13	Sycamore
Lid: centre panel	1 x 730 x 380 x 13	Sycamore
Lid: panels	2 x 100 x 380 x 13	Sycamore
Feet	4 x 240 x 70 x 60	Padauk
Lid: edge detail	2 x 520 x 22 x 10	Padauk
Handles (split turned)	2 x 80 x 22 Ø	Padauk
Chest bottom	1 x 1166 x 466 x 10	MDF/Ply
Drawer bottom	1 x 712 x 382 x 6	Ply

Padauk veneers for handle recess detail

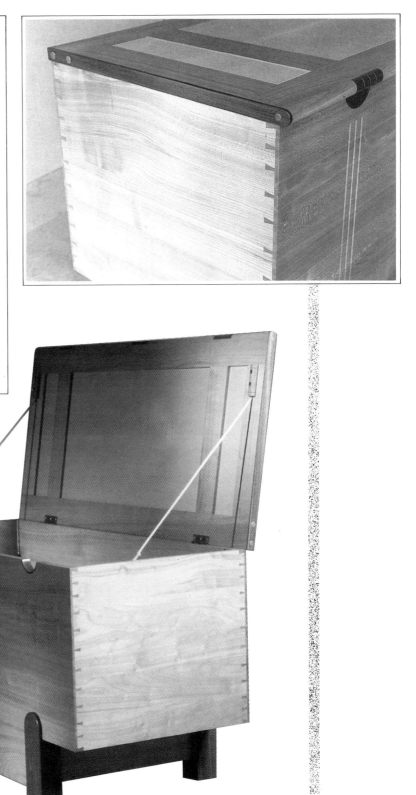

Completed chest

CORNER
CABINET

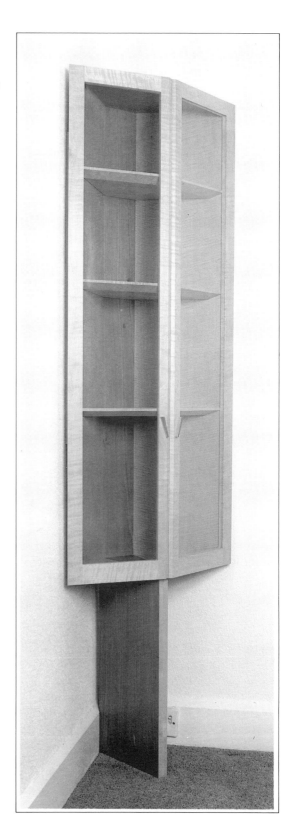

haven't often been asked to make corner cabinets, and must confess I have no great love for this furniture type. However, my objective was to produce a cabinet for storage and display of china and glass, with the structural clutter reduced to a minimum, and at the same time have a little fun with the form and techniques that seemed appropriate.

BASICS OF DESIGN

A large volume of storage space was not a primary requirement of this piece, nevertheless I wished to maximise the space available within a very small area. I therefore decided on a pentagonal plan, bringing the doors forward at 60° to the sides, and instead of a 90° back corner, a narrow flat panel, which affords an opportunity for a change of colour or material, giving a more distinctive background for the display. The cabinet is fixed to the wall by two screws through spacers on the sides, the heads of the screws hidden by the top shelf. The screws provide stability, while the weight of the cabinet is borne by a narrow plinth, the plan section of which is echoed as a decorative inlay on the inside of the bottom panel of the cabinet.

The materials used were 18mm MDF with solid sycamore lippings, various shades of grey dyed veneer, and solid rippled sycamore glazed door frames. Chipboard or plywood could be used as alternative substrates, chipboard being cheaper and plywood lighter than MDF. MDF was chosen as a dimensionally stable, reasonably cheap material, its main disadvantage being its considerable weight. It also provides a first-class surface for veneering.

LIPPING

After getting out the various panels of MDF the first job is lipping. Only the front edges of the side panels need this, the back edges forming a mitre joint with the back panel. The top and bottom (pentagonal) panels are fixed to the top and bottom edge of the sides, not inset, and are therefore relatively easy to cramp into position. This means their edges are exposed all round and thus need to be lipped all round.

In order not to expose the end grain the back lipping is applied first, then trimmed, followed by the sides, those trimmed, and finally the front lippings, mitred at 75° at the centre. The thickness of the lippings is not critical provided there is sufficient material for cleaning up: veneer

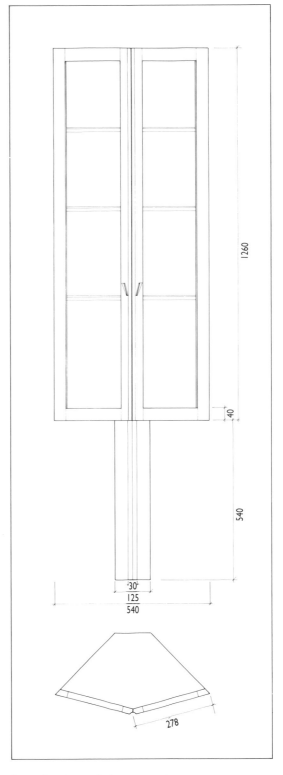

Front elevation and plan

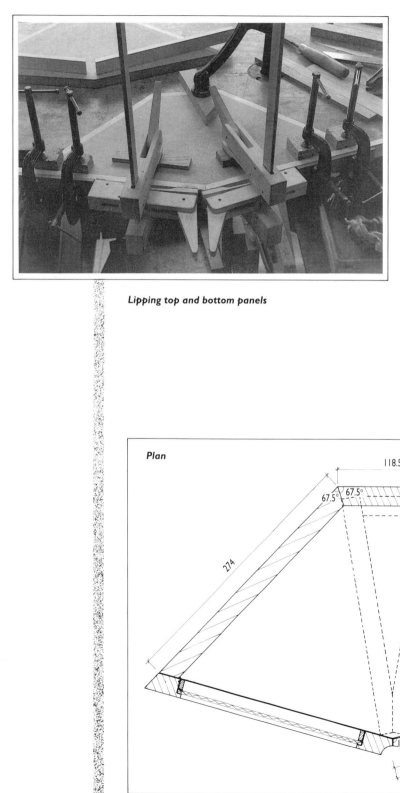

Lipping top and bottom panels

lippings, though much quicker and easier to apply, do not allow for any cleaning up after assembly, and in any case are rather too vulnerable to chipping.

VENEERING

The veneering is relatively straightforward, the narrow panels only requiring a single joint to be shot in the length. It may be possible to find veneer wide enough not to require jointing at all, but the bookmatched pattern of the figured veneer provided a pleasing lift to what might otherwise be a rather bland panel. To shoot the joints I support the pack of veneers between two pieces of ply cramped to the bench, using a foreplane on its side to plane an exact straight edge. The joint is then taped together using Sellotape or a similar low-tack clear tape. Paper veneer tape isn't always easy to get hold of, and without the proper applicators is extremely awkward to use. Sellotape is tricky stuff to remove after pressing (though this can be done most effectively using water, which wrinkles up the tape, and then cellulose thinners to dissolve the adhesive), but it has the advantage of being cheap, easily available and naturally elastic, which enables it to pull the joint tight.

Butt the veneers up to each other and rub half of a 75mm strip of tape on to the first piece, then stretch the

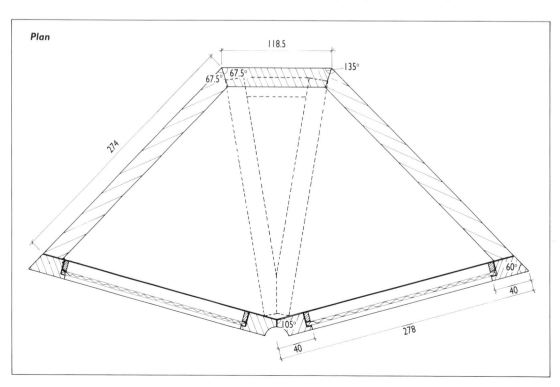

Plan

118.5

67.5° 67.5° 135°

274

60°

40

105°

40

278

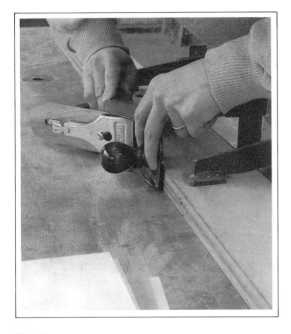

Shooting veneers

Cramping blocks in place

remainder over on to the opposite piece before rubbing down hard. The clear tape also allows inspection of the joint. I usually tape the joint in this way every 75mm or so, then rub a piece over the entire length of the joint and finally across the ends, to prevent cracking during handling and pressing.

GLUES

Pressing itself is obviously best done in a purpose-made veneer press, but such relatively small panels are easily cramped between cauls. In either case use paper or polyethylene sheet to prevent the glue squeeze-out sticking the panels to the cauls.

I would recommend the use of a UF resin such as Cascamite for veneering. Though there are many PVA resins made specifically for veneering in industry, general-purpose PVA can be a real problem. It has a relatively short assembly time, and subsequently when applying moisture to remove the tape it allows the veneer to buckle. In this case Cascamite is cheaper, stronger and less panic-inducing – all good enough reasons on their own to use the stuff. I allow 20 grams dry weight per square foot, which helps avoid unnecessary wastage of glue.

The mixed glue is best applied with a roller, though a spreader or brush will also do the job, if somewhat less

evenly. Do not be tempted to apply glue to the veneer – *it* will curl up, but *you* won't be laughing. Neither should the panel be awash with glue. Apart from giving yourself extra work cleaning up squeeze-out, you risk excessive glue penetration, particularly when using open-grained veneers such as oak or ash. Burrs are particularly susceptible to this problem, which can affect subsequent finishing. The side panels are veneered on the inside with figured enigre, dyed a silvery grey. The back panel is a dark blue-grey inside and all three have plain sycamore balancers on the back.

I would usually allow a couple of millimetres on the overall dimension for cleaning up veneered panels. Once the side and back panels have been veneered and the tape cleaned off, the front edges are cleaned up straight and square, then the back edge mitre sawn and shot accurately with a plane. A protractor square, or at least a sliding bevel, is necessary to check the 67.5° angle. A constant check must be kept to ensure the respective widths of the back and sides are parallel. The top and bottom panels should be trimmed up, as I say, fractionally oversize all round, but absolutely identical. While trimming and mitring, offer up the side and back panels to the appropriate edges of the top and bottom panels. When the carcase is assembled, the top and bottom need to be fractionally proud of the sides, so their edges can be planed or scraped carefully down to the veneered faces.

ASSEMBLING THE JOINT

The mitre joint is biscuited or tongue and grooved. (There are KD fixings available which eliminate the difficult and time-consuming cramping that this joint requires, but they are difficult to get hold of and generally subject to minimum-order quantities of a thousand, so we shall resign ourselves to wrestling with more primitive methods for now.) The problem is to get cramping pressure at 90° to the joint. As there is nothing for a cramp to hold on to, we have to stick temporary blocks on, using the time-honoured method of inserting a strip of paper into the glue joint, which can be subsequently split off and cleaned up leaving no visible marks. Because of its short setting time I used Titebond (aliphatic resin glue) for this. Obviously the blocks are only as strong as the glue joint, but enormous cramping pressure is not necessary.

Once the mitre is glued (Cascamite this time to give more assembly time) and cured, the blocks removed and back faces cleaned up, the top and bottom edges should be planed level and biscuited, tongue and grooved or dowelled. If you have a shortage of sash cramps, this joint would be equally strong glued, screwed and plugged. When this jointing is done, assemble the carcase dry before marking-out and cutting-in any inlay you might decide to use.

Assembly of side and back panels

Assembly of plinth

Template for marking out and cutting inlaid panel

Biscuiting underside panel for plinth fixing

Plan of plinth

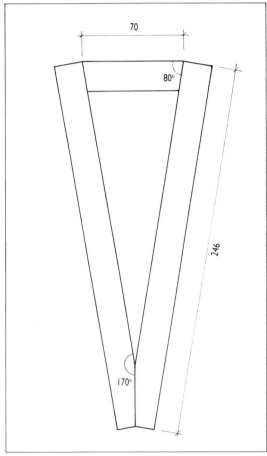

INLAID PANEL

As mentioned earlier, I inlaid a dark grey veneer into the silver grey of the inside bottom panel, the inlay being the plan of the plinth. On the inside front edges of the top I used dark grey bandings, again to emphasise and define the form. The banding was simply applied, the edge rebated to slightly less than the thickness of the veneer.

For the bottom section I made a hardboard template to both cut the veneer and knife-in the exact outline on to the panel. Not strictly necessary, but a method that makes an accurate fit all but foolproof. Most of the waste was then freehand routed away and the edges pared back to the knife line.

PLINTH ASSEMBLY

It is best if the plinth is made up before assembling the carcase to facilitate the jointing between the two. The back panel of the plinth is veneered, then fixed to the sides with a biscuited, angled-butt joint. This produces the wedge-shaped section. The sycamore lipping contrasts with the dark grey sides, expressing the veneered construction. The angle at which the two front edges meet is so shallow that it is best set out from a full-size drawing which enables all angles to be measured and checked. A simple means of setting out the angle as it appears here is to gauge 25mm in from the front edge, then 4mm from the inside edge. Plane down to these lines and the chamfer should be 170mm.

This joint needs no biscuit or tongue but is simply glued and butted. The internal angle, created by the conjunction of the two front edges, seemed an appropriate detail to make a feature of, though it can be treated in various ways.

Once the plinth assembly is complete, the top edges are marked out for biscuiting. Those marks are then transferred to the underside of the carcase bottom prior to cutting the joints. Work on the carcase can now be resumed. Sanding is very much more easily done at this stage, and if polishing by hand (as opposed to spraying) it is worth pre-finishing the inside faces.

Of course you will need to exercise special care of the finished surfaces after assembly, but they are not especially vulnerable and the time saved cutting back into awkward corners is well worth that effort. The top and bottom can now be glued on, after which all edges can be shot flush.

MAGIC WIRES

The carcase is now ready for shelves and doors. The shelves are in solid sycamore, deeply chamfered on the front edge and mounted on magic wires. Simple to fit, extremely strong and completely invisible, these shelf supports have a lot to recommend them. All they need is four 3mm holes appropriately spaced for each shelf, and a 3mm stopped groove routed into the shelf edge.

Cylindrical magnetic catches

Gluing on top and bottom panels

DOORS

The door frames have been kept as fine as possible bearing in mind the disconcerting tendency of stripped-up sycamore to bow and twist as soon as you look at it. It is definitely lively stuff, so try and choose as straight-grained boards as possible.

The length and position of the long and short shoulder mortise and tenon joints need to be carefully considered in order to avoid their being exposed inadvertently when the edges are angled and the central coving worked. When assembling the frames be particularly careful to avoid twist. Once they are glued the angle on the hinging edge can be worked, then the frame offered up to the carcase and the position of the closing edge marked from the central point. The butt hinges are let in in the usual way. (It irritates me that I have yet to find a British-made hinge that does not require hours of fettling with files and emery cloth in order to make it look halfway respectable.)

The coving detail is routed only when the doors are hung and fitted perfectly. Because of the inevitable problems of cutting against the grain in rippled sycamore it was necessary to grind up a special scraper and reshape a sanding block to clean up this detail.

The 3mm glass is fixed with sycamore beading pinned into the rebates, mitred at the corners. Cylindrical magnetic catches are let in top and bottom, either side of the centre point. It pays not to use magnets rated at more than a 2kg pull, otherwise the light frame tends to distort.

Detail of the door pulls

dramatically when pulled open. Lastly the pulls are veneered on the top surface, shaped and fixed using two screws in each. Something like 20mm 4s counterbored and plugged will do the job.

Once the doors are completed the plinth can be fixed. This is greatly facilitated by the use of deep-throated speed cramps, enabling pressure to be applied precisely where it is needed with very little trouble. Check the squareness of the plinth sides to the base carefully though.

Finally, the spacers which allow the onset doors room to function must be screwed to the outside face of the sides, while another is necessary to accommodate the wall-fixing screw.

Taking a deep breath and looking back over this, it seems an awful lot of work. This for the good and sufficient reason that it *is* a lot of work. As with all of these projects, however, I would encourage a careful, personal approach commensurate with your level of skill, time available, equipment etc. For instance, I could see this piece working very well using ply for the carcase and plinth, maybe using a coloured veneer lipping for contrast and only using solid timber in the doors and shelves. I could of course go on, but the design as drawn does provide an excellent starting point for modification and purposeful play.

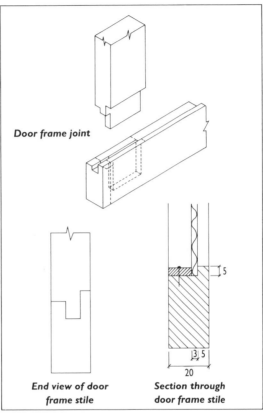

Door frame joint

End view of door frame stile

Section through door frame stile

Detail drawings for Corner Cabinet

Fixing plinth

CUTTING LIST

Side panels (assuming 20mm lipping)
2 x 1224 x 246 x 18 MDF

Back panel
1 x 1224 x 118.5 x 18   MDF

Top and bottom panel (assuming 10mm lipping)
2 x 485 x 235 x 18 MDF

Plinth (assuming 20mm lipping on front back and bottom edges)
Sides 2 x 520 x 208 x 18   MDF
Back 1 x 520 x 70 x 18   MDF

Shelves
3 x 460 x 230 x 18   Sycamore

Doors
Stiles   4 x 1260 x 40 x 20
Rails   4 x 275 x 40 x 20

I would recommend drawing a full-size plan section of both the carcase and the plinth, which will greatly facilitate accurate marking

COATSTAND

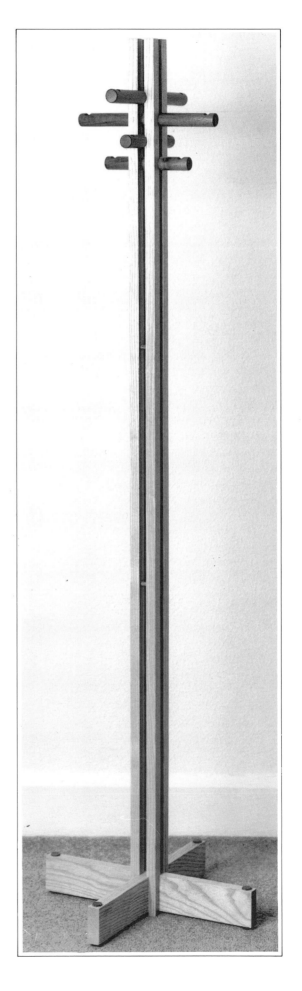

This is a relatively simple piece to make, though as usual success depends upon accuracy. The basic concept is also capable of considerable reinterpretation according to personal preferences, and I think I have proved this (to myself at least) by making several different versions since this original. In a way it is a perfect vehicle for a playful reworking of the original concept as it is essentially a very simple object. All sorts of different sections and colours could be used successfully and might result in a much more dramatic piece.

The material needs to be straight grained and resilient. In this case I used ash for the uprights and stand, English walnut for the 'hooks' and details.

Close-up of the cross piece

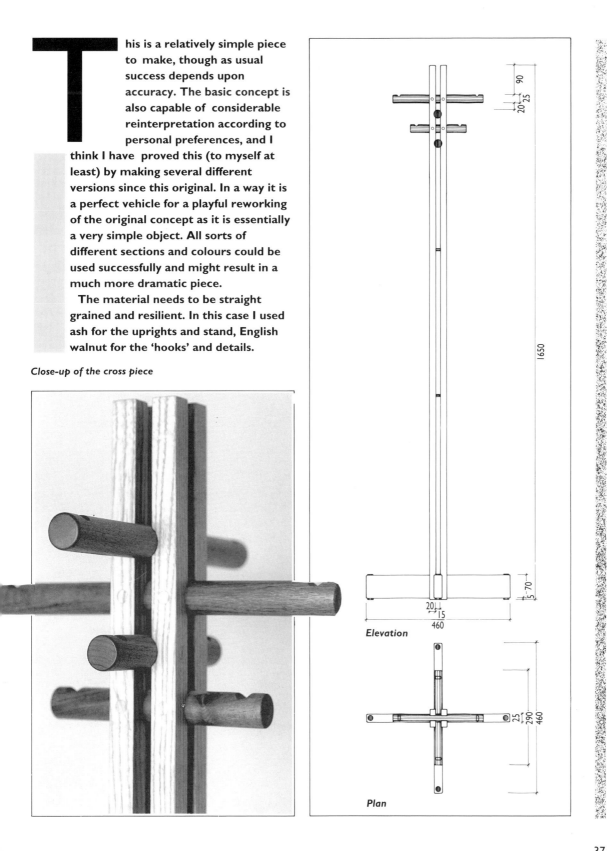

Elevation

Plan

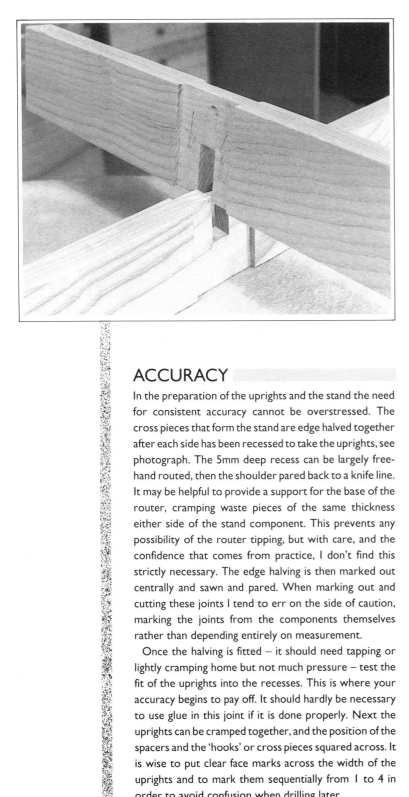

Stand: cross halving showing recesses for uprights

SPACERS

The spacers were of walnut turned to a straight 8mm cylinder, but size and configuration are a matter of personal choice. Tube type plug cutters are invaluable for producing this kind of component quickly. Possible alternatives are stained dowel or metal tube or bar – the drawing shows the method used here. If no lathe is available, either wooden or metal rod might be used, otherwise square-sectioned timber is equally appropriate as it can be related to the design of the stand.

ACCURACY

In the preparation of the uprights and the stand the need for consistent accuracy cannot be overstressed. The cross pieces that form the stand are edge halved together after each side has been recessed to take the uprights, see photograph. The 5mm deep recess can be largely free-hand routed, then the shoulder pared back to a knife line. It may be helpful to provide a support for the base of the router, cramping waste pieces of the same thickness either side of the stand component. This prevents any possibility of the router tipping, but with care, and the confidence that comes from practice, I don't find this strictly necessary. The edge halving is then marked out centrally and sawn and pared. When marking out and cutting these joints I tend to err on the side of caution, marking the joints from the components themselves rather than depending entirely on measurement.

Once the halving is fitted – it should need tapping or lightly cramping home but not much pressure – test the fit of the uprights into the recesses. This is where your accuracy begins to pay off. It should hardly be necessary to use glue in this joint if it is done properly. Next the uprights can be cramped together, and the position of the spacers and the 'hooks' or cross pieces squared across. It is wise to put clear face marks across the width of the uprights and to mark them sequentially from 1 to 4 in order to avoid confusion when drilling later.

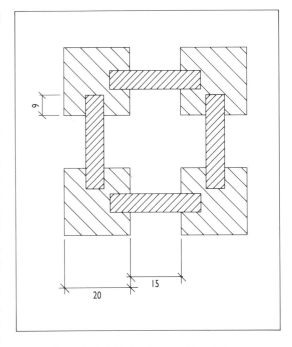

Section through uprights to show position of spacers

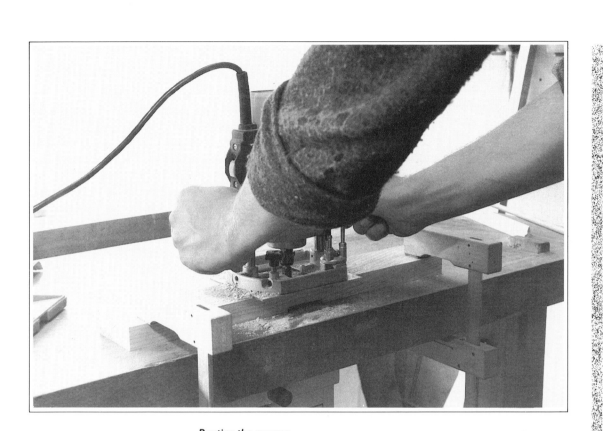

Routing the recesses

Drilling the uprights for the cross pieces

CROSS PIECES

The cross pieces, which are best turned, were in fact made with a rounding plane or rounder. This useful tool operates a little like a large pencil sharpener but, rather than a taper, produces a consistent and clean-cut cylinder from prepared stock. Available in various sizes, the tools have their limitations but are occasionally invaluable. Again, in the absence of either a rounder or a lathe, readily available dowelling would be perfectly acceptable.

The cross pieces were made to a diameter of 25mm, and the locating notches in the uprights were cut using a 25mm saw tooth or Forstner bit. This is possibly the most critical process of the construction in that it requires careful setting up and double-checking of both levelness and squareness. Make a couple of packing pieces 200 x 55 x 15mm to act as spacers while drilling. Cramp the uprights together with the packing piece, lining up the previously squared cross piece positions. Having centred the bit, drill through the packing piece to form the notches, taking care to support the grain as the bit breaks

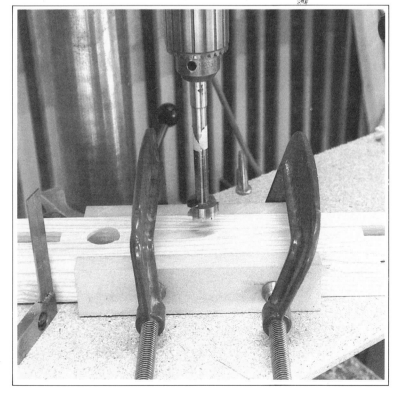

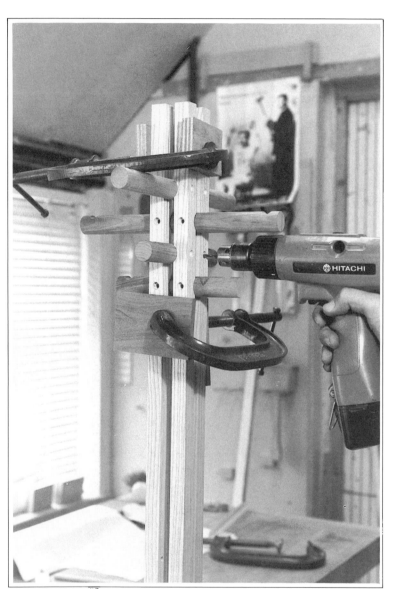

Cross piece assembly: drilling pilot holes for screw fixing

Jig for boring round notch in cross piece. The size and position of the smaller hole is optional.

through. This process is repeated in the appropriate positions for the other cross pieces.

The half round notches at the ends of the cross pieces (the coat hooks) can be worked in various ways – drilled in a suitable holding jig, see drawing, routed, or simply and quickly worked by hand using round files and dowel wrapped in abrasive paper.

The cross pieces are screwed to the uprights, the screws counterbored and plugged. This method allows for pre-finishing the components and means that glue is not needed. The counterboring and clearance holes are marked and drilled separately and the pilot holes drilled with the constituent parts cramped together. For the sake of symmetry, I screwed through each upright into

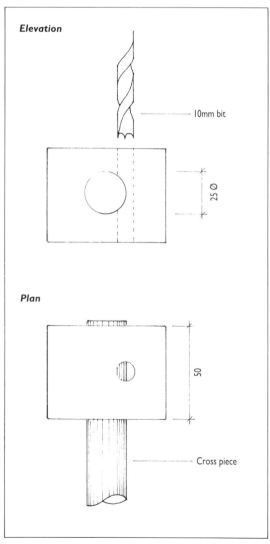

the cross piece from both sides, though it is possible to screw from one upright through to its opposite number and simply put a false plug on the latter.

INLAY

The stand was detailed with inlaid sections of walnut, cut with a 19mm plug cutter, to form feet which projected 5mm on the underside. To create the illusion of this section penetrating the width of the stand, the top edges were also inlaid with similar sections projecting 2mm. These details need to be let in by about 10mm and very gently tapped into the glued hole.

When cleaning up and sanding, be careful not to affect the fit of the cross pieces to the uprights and the uprights to the stand. Glue up the cross-halved stand before assembling the rest. The order of final assembly is:

1 Spacers to uprights
2 Cross pieces to uprights
3 Uprights into previously assembled stand

CUTTING LIST

Finished sizes

Uprights	4 x 1650 x 20 x 20	Ash
Base	2 x 460 x 70 x 25	Ash
Cross pieces	2 x 290 x 25	Walnut
	2 x 180 x 25	Walnut
Spacers	8 x 28 x 8	Walnut

Close-up of stand

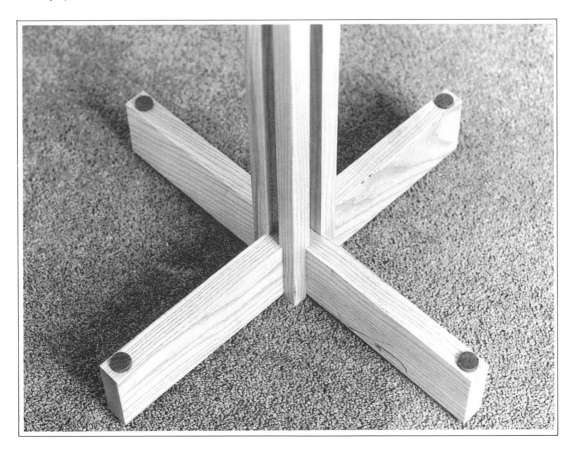

MIRROR

This straightforward frame design requires very little to be said of it. Intended as a companion piece (or even a counterpoint) to the coatstand previously described, it depends on proportion and simple moulded detail to enrich an otherwise rather bland wooden margin.

One note of caution, however. The mitres do need to be one hundred per cent accurate, as does the alignment of the flutes, or the point of the exercise will have been missed. Few things in wood construction announce themselves with such immediate and embarrassing effect as bad mitres.

MATERIALS

If bevelled glass is preferred, it is available from glass merchants in certain standard sizes. These should be checked in the workshop and related to the dimensions of the frame, allowing approximately 1mm clearance all round the glass. Special sizes can be ground to order but are very expensive.

After initial preparation of the main part of the frame material (in this case quarter sawn ash) the lipping should be glued on. I used walnut in this case, to contrast with the

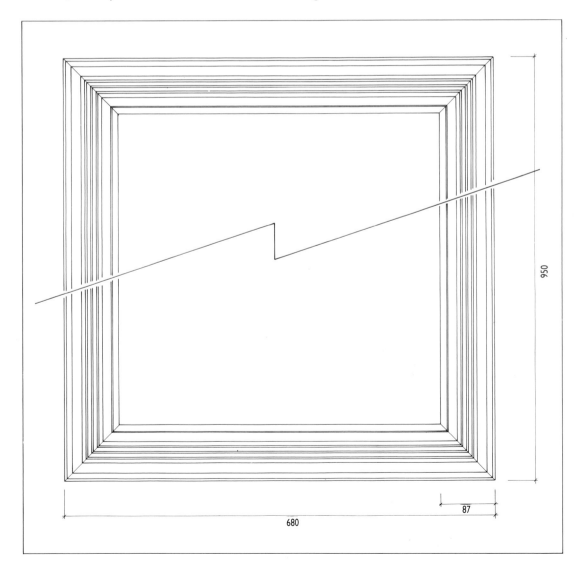

950

87

680

Corner detail

Framing showing lipping applied

paleness of the ash and to provide a stronger shadow line around the frame when mounted on a light-coloured wall. (I have made similar frames using the reverse effect, i.e. dark frame and light lipping, which works equally well.) The width of the lipping need only be little more than half the thickness of the edge, otherwise it will only be removed by the coving later.

MITRES

Now the mitres can be marked (cramp the opposite pairs of stiles/rails together to ensure exactly equal lengths when marking) and then cut. There are many different ways to do this, and obviously your choice will depend on equipment available. Fine-tuned radial arm or dimension saw (with equally fine blades), disc sander, mitre guillotine (if you're lucky enough to own one) – all will do the job if properly prepared. A production process calls for one solution, but with just four to do I tend to rely on a hand plane and one of the simplest jigs in the workshop – the mitre shooting block cramped in the vice. These are often best made for the job and are most effective for shooting small mitre joints. This fairly substantial frame can easily be marked and shot, checking rigorously with both try and mitre square.

A mitre joint will almost invariably require some mechanical reinforcement , especially as in this case it has to take a considerable load. Tongue and groove, dowel, and biscuit joints will all serve, but in order to achieve maximum strength and glue area I used loose tenons made from 10mm ply. The mortises for these can be chopped out by hand if necessary but the operation is accomplished less violently and far more quickly with a hollow chisel mortiser.

Once these joints are completed, it is important that they are put together dry and the surfaces flushed off prior to routing the rebates and flutes.

REBATES

The rebates are machined using the portable router mounted in a table, the depth of the back rebate being determined by the thickness of the backing panel, in this case 4mm ply or hardboard.

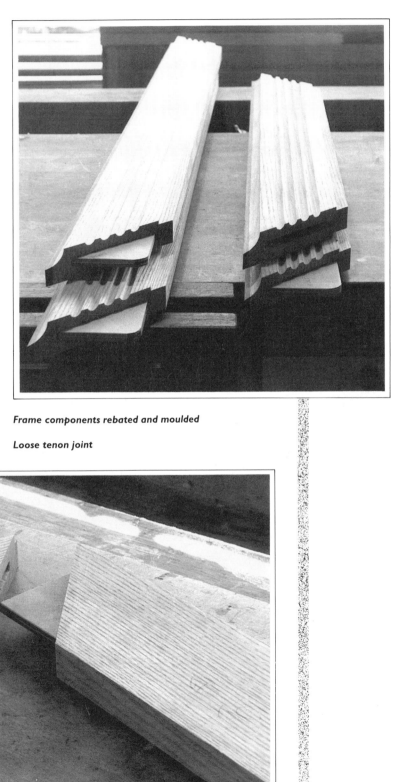

Frame components rebated and moulded

Loose tenon joint

FLUTES

The flutes are routed in the same way using a 6mm coving cutter. It is important to use a cutter that is in good condition, and to be both unrushed and confident in passing the wood over the machine. This is to minimise the hazards of tearing on the one hand, and burning on the other. If necessary the flutes can be cleaned up using a specially ground scraper – old hacksaw blade is ideal – and sanded with dowel wrapped with abrasive paper.

Strips of 12 x 6mm walnut are glued into the 5 x 4mm deep rebate on the inside edge of the face of the frame. This forms a raised detail which projects over the inner edge and provides a rebate for the mirror glass. A small chamfer was run round this – hardly more than a softening of the outer edge, but which nevertheless mediates between the contrasting materials. Once glued into the rebate the small mitre can be planed using the existing mitre as a guide for the heel of the plane.

CLEANING

It will pay to do preliminary cleaning up prior to gluing up the frame, even though some marking and glue squeeze-out are almost inevitable during assembly.

Although in making this particular frame I routed the coving on the edge at this stage, with the benefit of

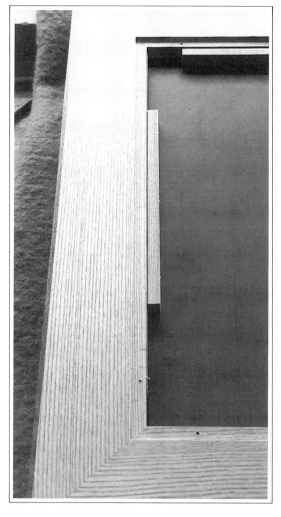

Spacer blocks being pinned

Back face of frame showing double rebate

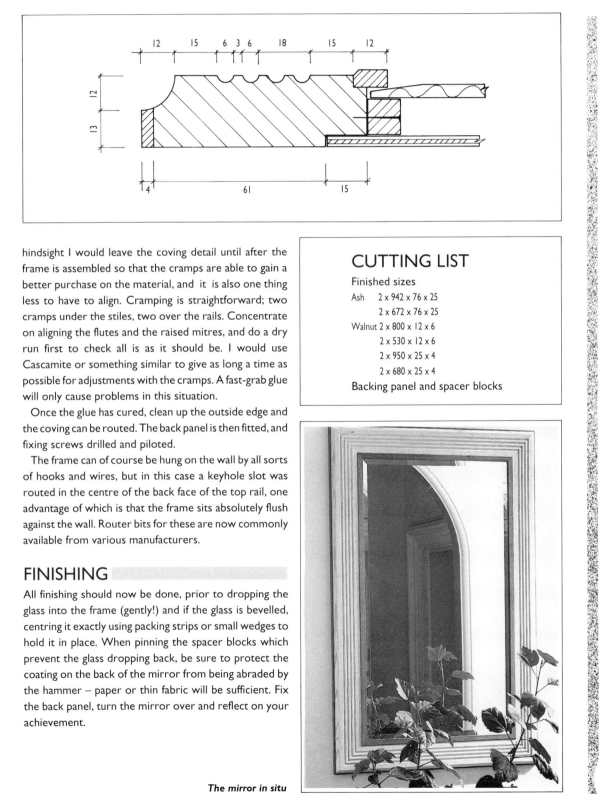

hindsight I would leave the coving detail until after the frame is assembled so that the cramps are able to gain a better purchase on the material, and it is also one thing less to have to align. Cramping is straightforward; two cramps under the stiles, two over the rails. Concentrate on aligning the flutes and the raised mitres, and do a dry run first to check all is as it should be. I would use Cascamite or something similar to give as long a time as possible for adjustments with the cramps. A fast-grab glue will only cause problems in this situation.

Once the glue has cured, clean up the outside edge and the coving can be routed. The back panel is then fitted, and fixing screws drilled and piloted.

The frame can of course be hung on the wall by all sorts of hooks and wires, but in this case a keyhole slot was routed in the centre of the back face of the top rail, one advantage of which is that the frame sits absolutely flush against the wall. Router bits for these are now commonly available from various manufacturers.

FINISHING

All finishing should now be done, prior to dropping the glass into the frame (gently!) and if the glass is bevelled, centring it exactly using packing strips or small wedges to hold it in place. When pinning the spacer blocks which prevent the glass dropping back, be sure to protect the coating on the back of the mirror from being abraded by the hammer – paper or thin fabric will be sufficient. Fix the back panel, turn the mirror over and reflect on your achievement.

CUTTING LIST

Finished sizes

Ash   2 x 942 x 76 x 25
        2 x 672 x 76 x 25
Walnut 2 x 800 x 12 x 6
        2 x 530 x 12 x 6
        2 x 950 x 25 x 4
        2 x 680 x 25 x 4
Backing panel and spacer blocks

The mirror in situ

COMPUTER DESK AND DRAWER UNIT

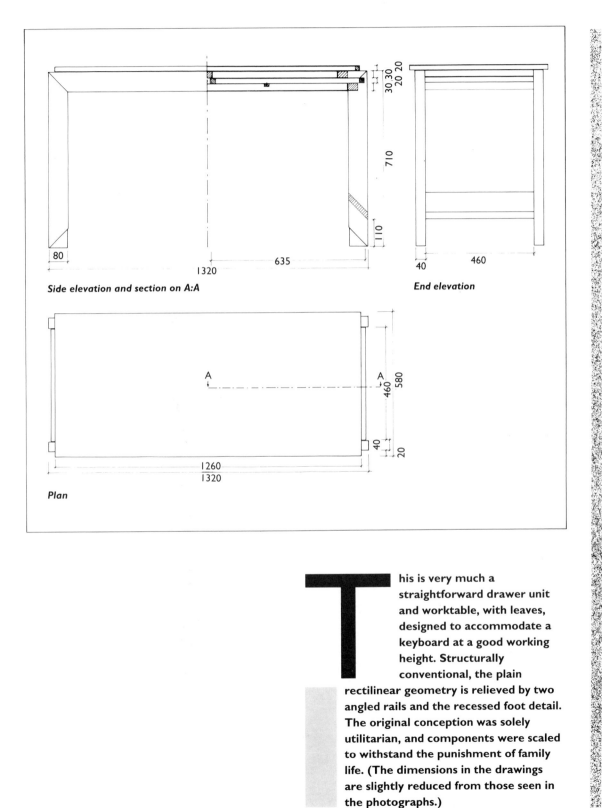

Side elevation and section on A:A

End elevation

Plan

This is very much a straightforward drawer unit and worktable, with leaves, designed to accommodate a keyboard at a good working height. Structurally conventional, the plain rectilinear geometry is relieved by two angled rails and the recessed foot detail. The original conception was solely utilitarian, and components were scaled to withstand the punishment of family life. (The dimensions in the drawings are slightly reduced from those seen in the photographs.)

Mitre joints and twin loose tenons

DESK PREPARATION

After preparing the timber to size, make the two main leg frames, which are mitred together. The joints are reinforced by twin loose tenons in each mitre, either of ply or solid wood. On such a long mitre extra reinforcement is essential. Dowelling could be considered as an alternative, but I would not advise succumbing to the temptations of ease and speed offered by biscuiting, as the strength of the finished joint would be less than adequate.

After assembling and cleaning up the front and back frames, the top cross rails are stub tenoned in. The distance between the bottom edge of the upper rail and the top edge of the lower rail will be determined by the total thickness of the finished panel (or leaf) that runs between them. I have shown it as a lipped 19mm MDF panel covered on the top side with linoleum approximately 1mm thick.

The lower of the top rails performs the function of a drawer rail, but is set back to allow the front edge of the leaf to oversail and form a sufficient finger grip.

The bottom rails, between the legs, are set at a 45° angle and dowelled. Stub tenons or stopped housings could be used here, but would be time-consuming both to mark and cut, while biscuits would not provide the same strength in shear as dowels. Leave the edges of the rails at 90° until the joint has been cut and the rail assembled dry to the legs. The angled edges can then be scribed and planed flush.

The foot detail consists of a 3mm deep recess routed and pared away, then overlaid with a contrasting veneer. My intention here was to provide a visual lift to an otherwise severely rectilinear composition, which was consonant with the angles of the lower rail and mitre joints. Of course all sorts of personal variations are possible.

Assembling the desk

Leaves, showing runner and stops

MAKING UP

Assembly of the underframe really needs two pairs of hands, and I would advise (as usual) meticulous preparation of the cramps and blocks before the glue starts to fly. Strips are screwed to the inside of the frame to form runners and kickers for the leaves. A stop is screwed to the underside of the leaves to limit the projection to approximately 300mm beyond the edges of the legs, which provides sufficient cantilever support within the framework for the most enthusiastic keyboard basher.

A centre stop is also screwed to the inside of the front or back rails to prevent one leaf pushing the other out if it is shut with too much force.

TOP

The top is an MDF panel, lippings mitred and, like the leaves, covered in linoleum. This is cut slightly oversize and then laid with contact adhesive, before being trimmed back using a router cutter with guide bearing. Finally, it is arrised with abrasive paper.

This is only the most direct method of finishing the panels; possibly a more visually 'finished' way would be to use exposed and mitred lippings all round, which would

Bottom rail joint and foot detail

work well with the mitres in the framing. However, it would necessitate a great deal of care when trimming back the lippings to the lino and generally take a lot more time.

FINISHING

The finish will depend largely on what material has been chosen, and the kind of use/abuse the piece might be expected to receive. In this case I used American ash, which was oiled prior to being liming waxed to emphasise the contrast between the white wood framing and black surfaces.

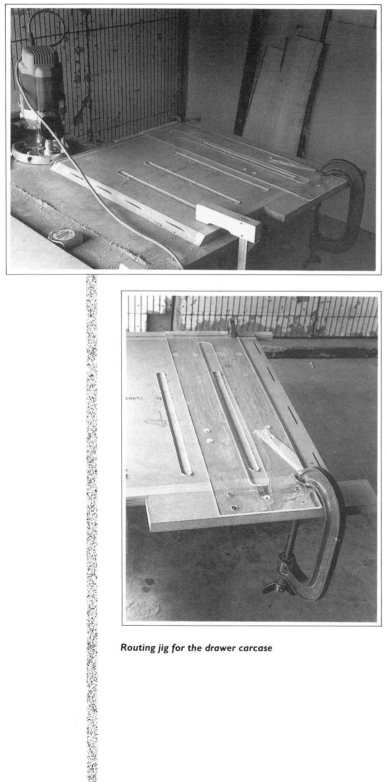

Side panel nearing completion

Routing jig for the drawer carcase

DRAWER UNIT

The mobile drawer unit was designed with flexibility in mind, and provides a further working surface as well as storage. Again, it is a workhorse, not sculpture, although the offset pulls give enough visual incident to rescue the piece from being too plain.

CARCASE

The carcase is lipped MDF, mitred at the top, butted at the bottom, and biscuited in each case. The base panel is set forward at the back to allow a 6mm ply back panel to be grooved in. It is well known that making drawers in a traditional manner is a time-consuming, and therefore expensive, activity. There are legitimate short cuts, but as this job was to some extent a teaching exercise, most of the techniques used are more or less textbook. With the carcase constructed from stable material and braced by the back panel, it was not strictly necessary to use all those drawer rails – the drawers could have been side-hung or even mounted on metal slides (the only way to absolutely guarantee a wooden drawer won't ever stick ... that, however, is another story), but this is an exercise in making traditionally run dovetailed drawers.

DRAWERS

The drawer rails are stub tenoned into the side panels, with the runners housed, barefaced, in behind. To rout the housing a T-square-type jig (see photograph) is especially useful. It consists of a sheet of 4mm acrylic, though ply would do, sufficiently wide to support the base of the router, and screwed to a stock of any convenient material.

Gauge a centre line on to the acrylic and rout a slot corresponding exactly to a conveniently sized guide bush. The centre line is then aligned with the centre lines of the housing marked on the panel, the jig is cramped and the housing routed using the appropriate guide bush. The

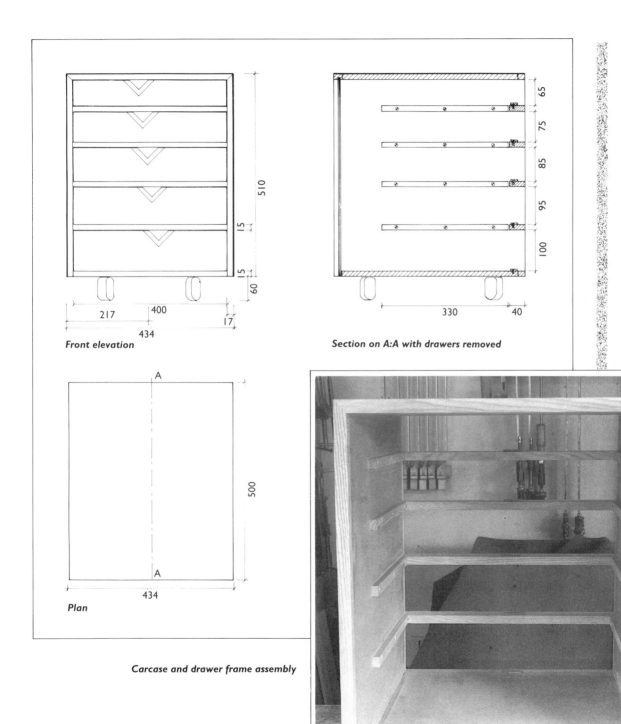

Front elevation

510

15

15

60

217

400

17

434

Section on A:A with drawers removed

65

75

85

95

100

330

40

A

A

500

434

Plan

Carcase and drawer frame assembly

Pull detail

housing need only be 3mm deep and doesn't need to extend right to the back of the cabinet. The runner is planed to fit exactly and is screw fixed. (It is not necessary to glue, nor to joint, the runner to the drawer rail.)

If flushing off the drawer rails and runners is necessary, do it before final assembly as far as possible. There are few things as dispiriting as struggling with a shoulder plane in a restricted opening – or as painful on the knuckles.

It's a good idea to fit drawer stops at this stage. They are very easy to forget, and are much easier fitted before assembly. A method I have found simple and effective is to glue a strip of thin ply or solid wood to a dowel. The drawer rail is drilled to take the dowel, which is not glued, allowing the stop to be withdrawn and the front edge (which contacts the back face of the drawer front) planed to provide the required fit.

The drawers are lap dovetailed at the front, through dovetailed at the back, and a ply bottom grooved in under the back in the usual way. Before assembling the drawers, the pulls are cut and the recess routed. The recess is inlaid with veneer, as for the foot detail on the worktable.

The sides, top and back panel are overlaid with linoleum, while the drawer fronts and carcase lippings are finished as for the table. Finally, castors are fixed to the base.

This scheme as a whole leaves considerable leeway for individual interpretation in terms of structure, capacity and decoration. It is best used as a starting point only, not a rigid plan.

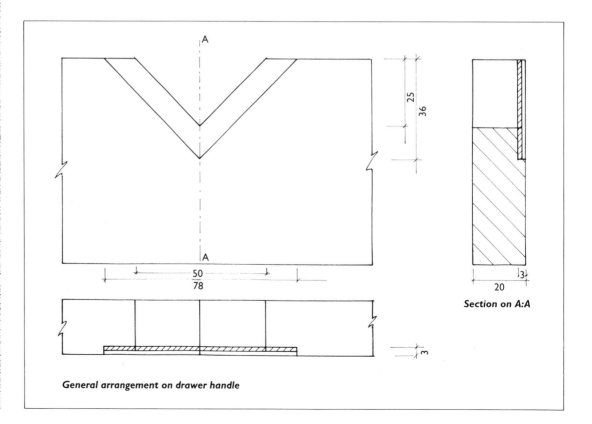

Section on A:A

General arrangement on drawer handle

CUTTING LIST

Finished sizes

Ash or similar timber is used

Legs	4 x 710 x 80 x 40
Long rails	2 x 1320 x 80 x 40
Cross rails	5 x 520 x 40 x 30
Bottom rails	2 x 520 x 130 x 20
Top lippings	2 x 1260 x 20 x 18
	2 x 580 x 20 x 18
Lower top lippings	4 x 595 x 20 x 18
	4 x 460 x 20 x 18
Top fillets	4 x 520 x 30 x 15
Lower fillets	2 x 1160 x 30 x 15
Central stop	2 x 30 x 30 x 20
Stops for sliding panels	2 x 350 x 20 x 10

Panels in MDF

Top panel	1 x 1220 x 540 x 18
Lower panels	2 x 595 x 420 x 18
Linoleum (1-2mm thick)	
Contrast veneer for handle and foot detail	

Panels in MDF

Top panel	1 x 430 x 500 x 15
Side panels	2 x 510 x 500 x 15
Bottom panel	1 x 400 x 488 x 15
Back panel	1 x 501 x 412 x 6
	(or ply)

Ash or similar timber

Drawer rails	4 x 420 x 40 x 15
Drawer runners	8 x 330 x 15 x 15
Drawer fronts	1 x 400 x 64 x 20
	1 x 400 x 75 x 20
	1 x 400 x 85 x 20
	1 x 400 x 95 x 20
	1 x 400 x 100 x 20
Drawer sides	2 x 450 x 65 x 10
	2 x 450 x 75 x 10
	2 x 450 x 85 x 10
	2 x 450 x 95 x 10
	2 x 450 x 100 x 10
Drawer backs	1 x 400 x 45 x 10
	1 x 400 x 55 x 10
	1 x 400 x 65 x 10
	1 x 400 x 75 x 10
	1 x 400 x 80 x 10
Drawer bottoms: plywood	5 x 434 x 388 x 4

Linoleum (1-2mm)

Contrast veneer

4 castors

A closer look at the drawers

INFORMAL FORM

This design reduces the structure to the simplest elements arranged in a very logical manner. The visual quality relies on the expression of the structure: the bracing rail becomes a part of the seat instead of supporting it, and the tenons are brought through, combining great strength with a visual punctuation, which though not essential, certainly enlivens the object. The seat is subtly dished which also helps rescue the piece from being flatly foursquare. The generosity of the section also contributes a great deal to the effect without being grossly extravagant.

It may be possible to find sufficient width in certain timbers for the leg without having to joint up panels from narrow boards. There are no special benefits to this, though work is reduced a little; in any case, much will depend on the capacity of your machines.

Once the legs are prepared the tenons are routed and sawn; exact size and position is not critical, but here they are 25mm square with a 20mm shoulder on the outside edge, leaving a 25mm oversail on the edge of the seat. The gap between the pairs of tenons is 15mm.

The seat boards should be prepared to slightly over-finished thickness and left rectangular in section while the mortises are cut. These should first be marked out and cut exactly square. It is best to mark out and work from both sides in order to avoid break out when cutting through mortises. When the mortises are cut thus, and the tenons fitted satisfactorily to them, they can be opened up by 2mm each side at the top, going down to nothing just short of the bottom of the joint. Make sure to do this on the end grain sides of the mortises as you will not appreciate the results of knocking in wedges in the long grain direction!

The tenons are sawn to take the wedges no more than 6mm from each side, and the cut should stop a little short of the shoulder line. The wedges should be at least 3mm longer than these saw cuts, and their maximum thickness should exceed the amount by which the mortise was

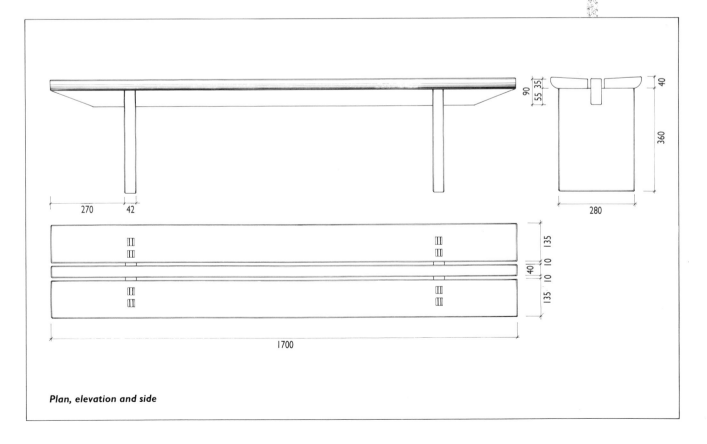

Plan, elevation and side

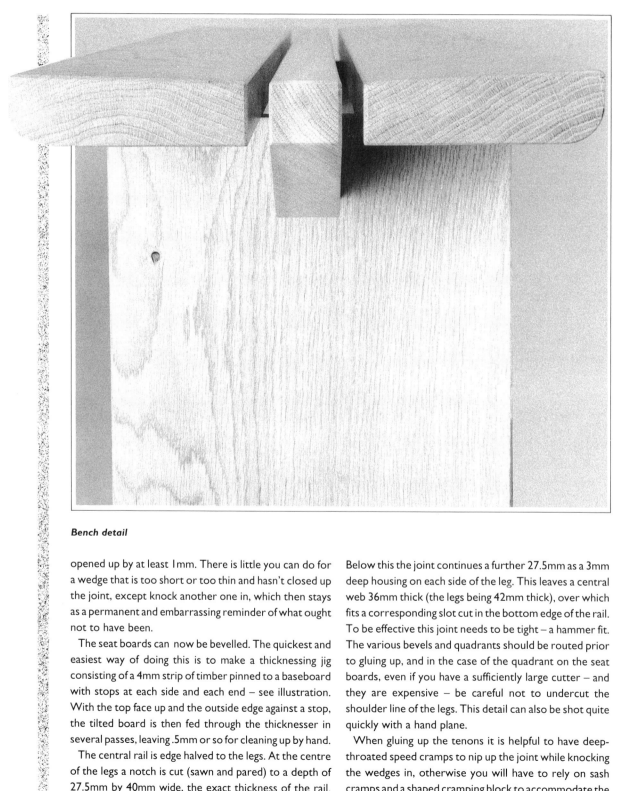

Bench detail

opened up by at least 1mm. There is little you can do for a wedge that is too short or too thin and hasn't closed up the joint, except knock another one in, which then stays as a permanent and embarrassing reminder of what ought not to have been.

The seat boards can now be bevelled. The quickest and easiest way of doing this is to make a thicknessing jig consisting of a 4mm strip of timber pinned to a baseboard with stops at each side and each end – see illustration. With the top face up and the outside edge against a stop, the tilted board is then fed through the thicknesser in several passes, leaving .5mm or so for cleaning up by hand.

The central rail is edge halved to the legs. At the centre of the legs a notch is cut (sawn and pared) to a depth of 27.5mm by 40mm wide, the exact thickness of the rail.

Below this the joint continues a further 27.5mm as a 3mm deep housing on each side of the leg. This leaves a central web 36mm thick (the legs being 42mm thick), over which fits a corresponding slot cut in the bottom edge of the rail. To be effective this joint needs to be tight – a hammer fit. The various bevels and quadrants should be routed prior to gluing up, and in the case of the quadrant on the seat boards, even if you have a sufficiently large cutter – and they are expensive – be careful not to undercut the shoulder line of the legs. This detail can also be shot quite quickly with a hand plane.

When gluing up the tenons it is helpful to have deep-throated speed cramps to nip up the joint while knocking the wedges in, otherwise you will have to rely on sash cramps and a shaped cramping block to accommodate the

CUTTING LIST

Finished sizes

Seat	2 x 1700 x 135 x 40	Oak
Rail	1 x 1700 x 90 x 40	Oak
Legs	2 x 400 x 280 x 42	Oak

Wedges in contrasting timber

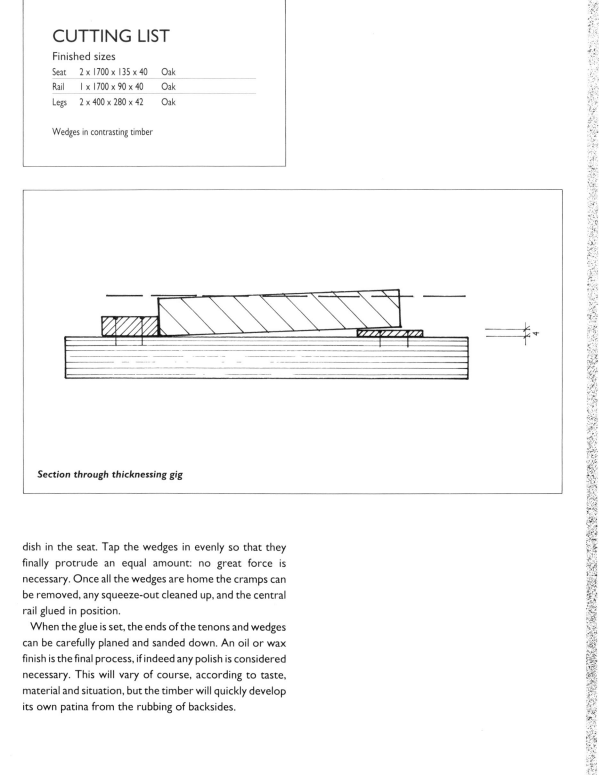

Section through thicknessing gig

dish in the seat. Tap the wedges in evenly so that they finally protrude an equal amount: no great force is necessary. Once all the wedges are home the cramps can be removed, any squeeze-out cleaned up, and the central rail glued in position.

When the glue is set, the ends of the tenons and wedges can be carefully planed and sanded down. An oil or wax finish is the final process, if indeed any polish is considered necessary. This will vary of course, according to taste, material and situation, but the timber will quickly develop its own patina from the rubbing of backsides.

WAVE BENCH

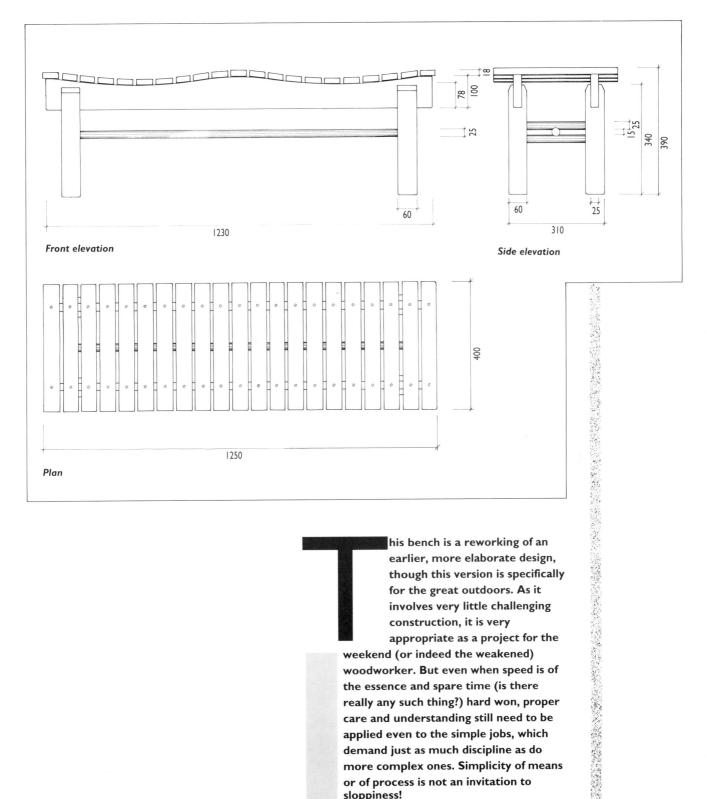

Front elevation

1230

60

18

78 100

25

Side elevation

15 25

340

390

60 25

310

400

Plan

1250

This bench is a reworking of an earlier, more elaborate design, though this version is specifically for the great outdoors. As it involves very little challenging construction, it is very appropriate as a project for the weekend (or indeed the weakened) woodworker. But even when speed is of the essence and spare time (is there really any such thing?) hard won, proper care and understanding still need to be applied even to the simple jobs, which demand just as much discipline as do more complex ones. Simplicity of means or of process is not an invitation to sloppiness!

TIMBER

I made this bench as a companion piece to a garden seat and used iroko – well known for its good weathering qualities. Teak is an option of course, when available, but very expensive. If nasal passages are inflamed by iroko dust (it is very peppery, and effective dust masks should certainly be worn when machining), or ecological principles offended by the use of tropical hardwoods, there are of course several home-grown alternatives, oak being the favourite. It will, however, cost three or four times as much. Suitably treated with microporous preservative, however, even softwoods will give many years' service.

PREPARATION

The legs, top rails and slats can all be planed to size and sawn to exact length.

While the top rails are still square and parallel, the stopped bridle joint should be set out and worked. The bridle on the legs is 20mm thick, requiring a 5mm recess to be routed on each side of the 30mm rails. Use the legs as a template to set out the width of the recess, square round with the marking knife, freehand rout to within 0.5mm of the line and clean up the shoulder by paring. The slots on the legs can now be sawn and fitted to the recesses.

A well-fitted joint should not need further reinforcement (once glued) but the joints can be either pinned or screwed (the latter from the inside) if desired.

Before gluing up, saw and plane the chamfers on the top of the legs and mark out and cut the curved top edges on the rails. This is most easily done by setting them out on a template of hardboard or similar material, though it can be done directly on to the rail. Mark the centres of the curves, the high and low points, and using a long steel rule or flexible wooden strip, spring the curve and scribe along the guide. Two pairs of hands are a help in doing this, but it's not impossible on your own. The advantage of using a template is that the symmetry of the curves can be checked, flipping the template end for end.

One marked, the rails can be bandsawn and routed from the template. Rail 2 can of course be marked and even routed from rail 1 using a following cutter, thus ensuring exact parallelism.

UNDERFRAMING

The underframing consists of two round rails, each end fitted in their full diameter into holes bored in the legs. The rails can be rounded by hand (laborious, but easily

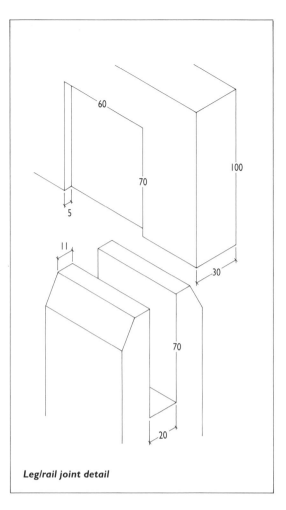

Leg/rail joint detail

possible with planes or rounders), routed or spindled. It all depends on the technology and/or time you have available. 25mm round section hardwood can be bought over the counter of course, but the materials tend to be limited to those commonly used for dowelling.

The long central bottom rail is notched between the two end rails to a depth of 5mm, thus leaving a 15mm gap between the end rails. The notch can be drilled, or routed very accurately in a suitable jig (similar to that used in making the Coatstand, page), but for so few joints the job is easily and effectively done with a half-round file.

Accurate marking out of the centres of the rails is essential, followed by drilling or filing of the recesses in the end rails – the long rail being left plain. If required the recesses can be cleaned up using abrasive paper wrapped around a section of the round rail.

ASSEMBLY

The H-frame is assembled before the end rails are glued into the legs. The long rail is fixed to the two cross rails at each end by gluing and screwing through from underneath. The drilling of the pilot is best done with the end rails in situ, i.e. partially entered into the holes in the legs. This will keep everything parallel and steady.

The assembly sequence begins with the legs to the top curved rails and should require no more than tapping home the bridle and pinching with a G-cramp on each joint. (Pinning or screwing can be done after glue has cured.) Assuming the bottom rail is already glued and screwed to the end rails, the H-frame as a whole can now be glued to the legs.

It only remains to screw-fix the slats to the curved top rails to complete the structure, though even here care should be exercised in order to achieve an even spacing. It is helpful to begin either in the middle, and work out towards each end, or the reverse, and to use a 10mm wide spacer to determine the gap between each slat. If you begin at one end and work towards the other, unless your calculations are perfect *and* your timber preparation is consistently faultless *and* your fixing absolutely spot on, you are extremely likely to end up with that last slat overhanging the end of the rail in a distinctly asymmetrical way. You may of course be just such a wonderful creature, but I wouldn't trust myself that far.

If you find the idea of exposed screw heads offensive (and I don't see why they should be, particularly if seated neatly in brass screw cups), the slats can be counterbored and plugged – possibly using a contrasting timber to make a decorative detail.

FINISH

I finished the bench with three coats of teak oil, though the microporous finishes already mentioned would be particularly appropriate for the less hardy timbers and are commonly available in a great variety of colours.

CUTTING LIST

Legs	4 x 340 x 60 x 60
Top rails	2 x 1230 x 100 x 30
Slats	21 x 400 x 50 x 18
End rails	4 x 270 x 25mm dia
Bottom rail	1 x 1130 x 25mm dia

NEST OF TABLES

This project is about simplicity. The structure is reduced to the barest minimum consonant with sufficient strength, but my objective was not merely to strip everything back to the bare bones. Rather, it was to achieve a satisfying whole dependent on carefully worked, logical details.

There are two major details: **1** the chamfering of the edges which allows the individual tables to be easily picked up and has a visually unifying effect when the three units are stored together; **2** the pinning of the mitre which is primarily a reinforcement of the joint but can be made into a decorative feature. This aspect is very much open to personal interpretation regarding both the placement and spacing of the pins and the material used.

In this example I have used wenge with stainless steel pins (4mm round bar) but again this is a matter of choice.

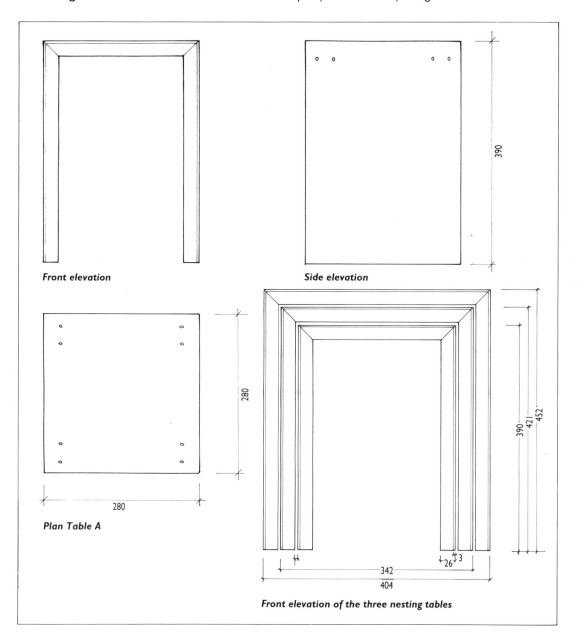

Front elevation

Side elevation

Plan Table A

Front elevation of the three nesting tables

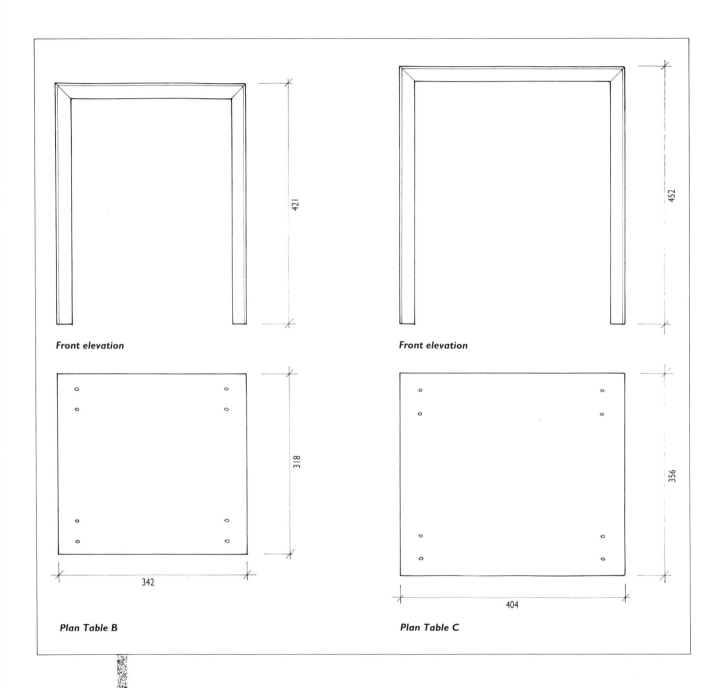

Front elevation

Front elevation

Plan Table B

Plan Table C

This design could work very well using quite different materials – ply, softwood, veneered board. A word of warning though – if you decide to use the idea but wish to change any dimensions, I would strongly recommend that you re-draw the set to make sure the relative sizes are correct, and in particular the chamfer lines up – see sectional drawing.

If you are using solid wood it should go without saying that this design demands well-seasoned and stable timber. Give that propeller-shaped piece of fruitwood you've saved in the garden shed a wide berth!

PREPARATION

Preparation is straightforward though it's worth trying to achieve a consistency of grain on each table if possible, especially if you have some interesting colour or figure in your timber. Ideally the tables should look as though they had just been folded from a single board. (This effect is of course quite easy to achieve using veneer.)

In solid wood, therefore, prepare material to make a board approximately 1380 x 360 x 26. This is for the largest (top) table – you can determine the dimensions for the others from the drawings. This allows for the cutting of mitres and trimming of ends – see drawing of Front Elevation.

It is only necessary to prepare a board of this length if the consistency of grain mentioned is considered to be essential. Otherwise shorter lengths of material to make up the various side and top pieces are quite adequate.

The mitres are best cut, as these were, on a circular saw with tilting arbor, though it is perfectly possible to do them by hand. If you have a circular saw but cannot rely on its accuracy, I recommend removing the majority of the waste and cleaning up with a finely set jack plane. This latter method will require marking out the individual pieces.

With an accurate table saw with a crosscut fence and end stop it is possible to do the whole job just by resetting the end stop for the various cuts.

As a circular saw will only tilt one way, the opposite edge of piece **A** will be against the fence to that of piece **C**, and similarly with either end of piece **B** (the top). The implications of this for machining are that it is essential that the pieces are absolutely parallel and the mitre cut dead square across the width, otherwise, when finally assembled, much grief will ensue.

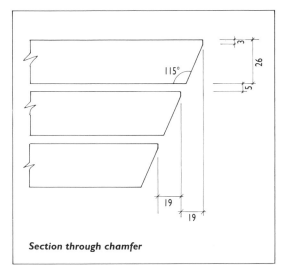

Section through chamfer

CHAMFERING

When the mitres are cut and the side pieces are to length, the chamfer can be worked. This is again best done on a circular saw, though with a rip blade this time as we are cutting with the grain. I repeat, the angle here depends on the dimensions of each table – if any of these are changed the angle of the chamfer changes.

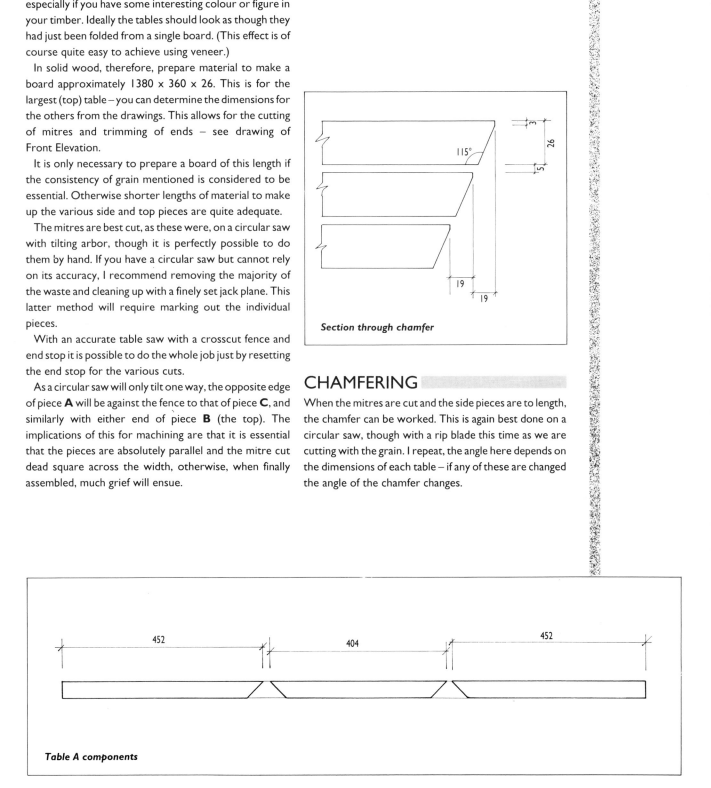

Table A components

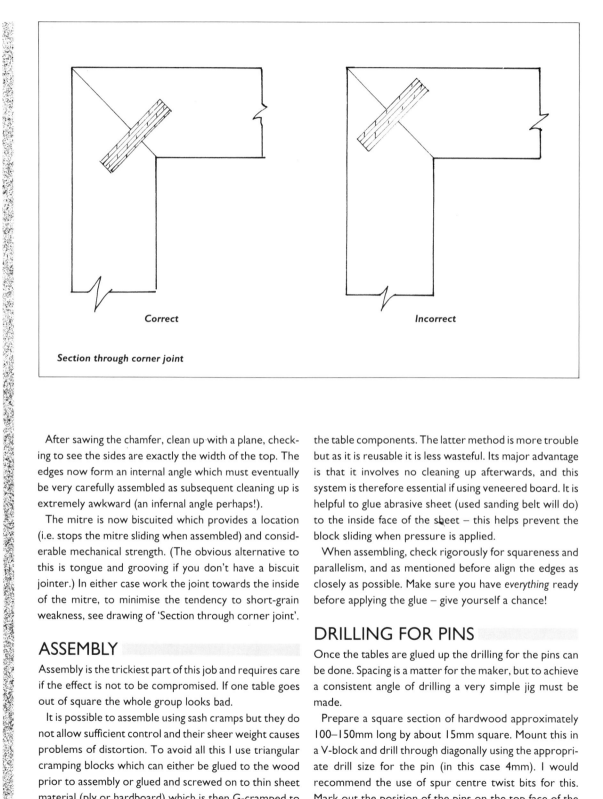

Correct

Incorrect

Section through corner joint

After sawing the chamfer, clean up with a plane, checking to see the sides are exactly the width of the top. The edges now form an internal angle which must eventually be very carefully assembled as subsequent cleaning up is extremely awkward (an infernal angle perhaps!).

The mitre is now biscuited which provides a location (i.e. stops the mitre sliding when assembled) and considerable mechanical strength. (The obvious alternative to this is tongue and grooving if you don't have a biscuit jointer.) In either case work the joint towards the inside of the mitre, to minimise the tendency to short-grain weakness, see drawing of 'Section through corner joint'.

ASSEMBLY

Assembly is the trickiest part of this job and requires care if the effect is not to be compromised. If one table goes out of square the whole group looks bad.

It is possible to assemble using sash cramps but they do not allow sufficient control and their sheer weight causes problems of distortion. To avoid all this I use triangular cramping blocks which can either be glued to the wood prior to assembly or glued and screwed on to thin sheet material (ply or hardboard) which is then G-cramped to

the table components. The latter method is more trouble but as it is reusable it is less wasteful. Its major advantage is that it involves no cleaning up afterwards, and this system is therefore essential if using veneered board. It is helpful to glue abrasive sheet (used sanding belt will do) to the inside face of the sheet – this helps prevent the block sliding when pressure is applied.

When assembling, check rigorously for squareness and parallelism, and as mentioned before align the edges as closely as possible. Make sure you have *everything* ready before applying the glue – give yourself a chance!

DRILLING FOR PINS

Once the tables are glued up the drilling for the pins can be done. Spacing is a matter for the maker, but to achieve a consistent angle of drilling a very simple jig must be made.

Prepare a square section of hardwood approximately 100–150mm long by about 15mm square. Mount this in a V-block and drill through diagonally using the appropriate drill size for the pin (in this case 4mm). I would recommend the use of spur centre twist bits for this. Mark out the position of the pins on the top face of the

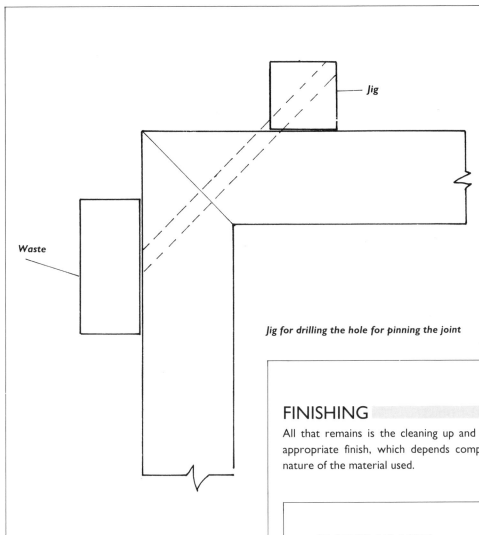

Jig

Waste

Jig for drilling the hole for pinning the joint

table and cramp the jig in place.

The jig will enable you to start the hole without skating and to maintain the correct angle. If the drill bit is not long enough to complete the hole, drill as far as possible, remove the jig and use the existing hole. As a precaution against break out, cramp some waste to the side of the table, see drawing.

If using metal pins glue in pre-cut lengths using epoxy adhesive. I have found the trimming of these best done with a handfile rather than power abrasion, which causes a rapid and dramatic build up of heat which does not improve the efficacy of the glue!

FINISHING

All that remains is the cleaning up and application of appropriate finish, which depends completely on the nature of the material used.

CUTTING LIST
Finished sizes

Small table
2 x 390 x 284 x 26
1 x 280 x 284 x 26
or (1 x 1040 x 284 x 26)

Medium table
2 x 421 x 322 x 26
1 x 342 x 322 x 26
or (1 x 1260 x 322 x 26)

Large table
2 x 452 x 360 x 26
1 x 404 x 360 x 26
or (1 x 1380 x 360 x 26)

GARDEN SEAT

When spring has sprung, a woodworker's fancy lightly turns to ... well, maybe the garden and returning some of his beloved material, suitably reworked, to the great outdoors. Wood is quite happy living outside. It requires intelligent – though straightforward – handling if it is to give good service, but so does timber destined for our superheated homes and offices, if in a quite different way.

The constraints governing the design of wooden outdoor furniture have, at least in England, generally resulted in objects remarkable chiefly for their stunning mediocrity. An extremely low aesthetic value prevails – one that is wooden in the most pejorative sense.

There are exceptions, thankfully. Possibly the most celebrated is the Lutyens seat. This, it must be said, is a fairly elaborate construction, especially for a piece of garden furniture, and there, I am sure, is the rub. In a country renowned for its forty-eight-hour summers, few people seem to feel it is worth investing , either as a consumer or as a maker, in something even marginally more beautiful than the cheapest, crudest bum-support available.

This seat was my first attempt, some years ago now, at designing for outdoors, and while far from being a perfect solution, it attempts to invest an ordinary object with sufficient presence for it to be able to contribute to the delight of a garden, and not, like a compost heap, be merely useful and best out of sight.

MATERIALS

There is a general consensus that teak is the most appropriate timber for making outdoor furniture because it is extremely stable and durable. It also looks handsome and contains enough natural oils not to require finishing. It is, in fact, very resistant to preservative treatment, although it does take oil well.

The downside of all this concern is cost and, to an extent, availability, not to mention ensuring the source of the timber is properly managed, i.e. renewable forest. The traditional substitute is iroko, which was used in this example. This waxy timber is approximately half the price of teak – unfortunately it is not pleasant to use. The grain is generally interlocked and the dust nastily noxious.

It is also perfectly legitimate to use more conventional timbers in conjunction with preservatives and weather-resistant finishes, particularly the microporous ones now commonly available. These also allow a wide range of colour options, but these will require regular maintenance.

The most important factor in choosing material is dimensional stability. For instance, if the top back rail were to be in oak, its width at centre could result in problems of movement and subsequent distortion.

The joint most commonly found in outdoor furniture construction is the pinned mortise and tenon, whereby the tenon is bored at right angles after the joint has been assembled and reinforced by one or more dowels. Apart from the decorative opportunity, this process acts as a kind of insurance against the possibility of ill-fitting joints (heaven forfend) and, more importantly, glue failure.

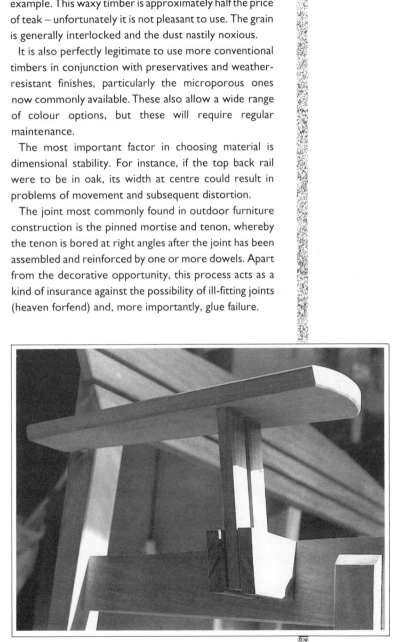

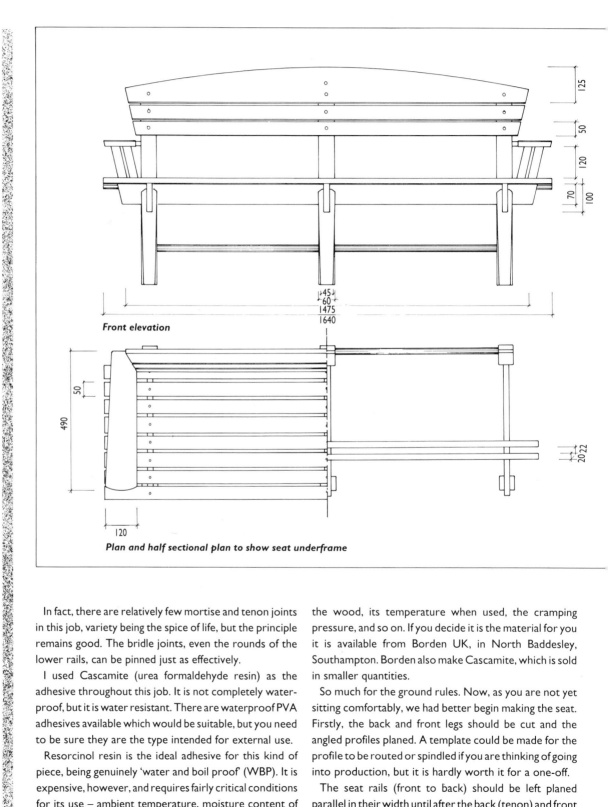

Front elevation

Plan and half sectional plan to show seat underframe

In fact, there are relatively few mortise and tenon joints in this job, variety being the spice of life, but the principle remains good. The bridle joints, even the rounds of the lower rails, can be pinned just as effectively.

I used Cascamite (urea formaldehyde resin) as the adhesive throughout this job. It is not completely waterproof, but it is water resistant. There are waterproof PVA adhesives available which would be suitable, but you need to be sure they are the type intended for external use.

Resorcinol resin is the ideal adhesive for this kind of piece, being genuinely 'water and boil proof' (WBP). It is expensive, however, and requires fairly critical conditions for its use – ambient temperature, moisture content of the wood, its temperature when used, the cramping pressure, and so on. If you decide it is the material for you it is available from Borden UK, in North Baddesley, Southampton. Borden also make Cascamite, which is sold in smaller quantities.

So much for the ground rules. Now, as you are not yet sitting comfortably, we had better begin making the seat. Firstly, the back and front legs should be cut and the angled profiles planed. A template could be made for the profile to be routed or spindled if you are thinking of going into production, but it is hardly worth it for a one-off.

The seat rails (front to back) should be left planed parallel in their width until after the back (tenon) and front

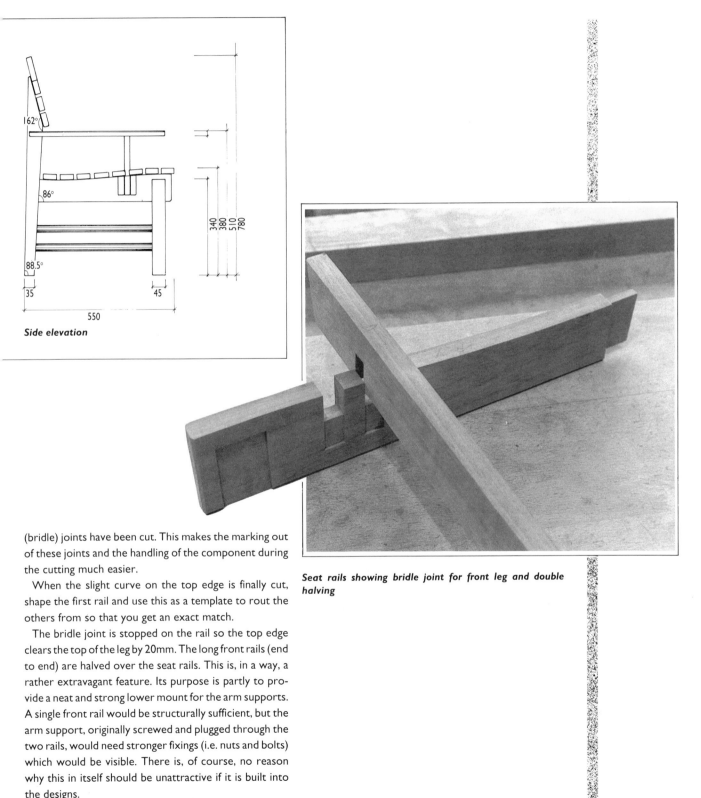

162°

86°

88.5°

35

45

340
380
510
780

550

Side elevation

Seat rails showing bridle joint for front leg and double halving

(bridle) joints have been cut. This makes the marking out of these joints and the handling of the component during the cutting much easier.

When the slight curve on the top edge is finally cut, shape the first rail and use this as a template to rout the others from so that you get an exact match.

The bridle joint is stopped on the rail so the top edge clears the top of the leg by 20mm. The long front rails (end to end) are halved over the seat rails. This is, in a way, a rather extravagant feature. Its purpose is partly to provide a neat and strong lower mount for the arm supports. A single front rail would be structurally sufficient, but the arm support, originally screwed and plugged through the two rails, would need stronger fixings (i.e. nuts and bolts) which would be visible. There is, of course, no reason why this in itself should be unattractive if it is built into the designs.

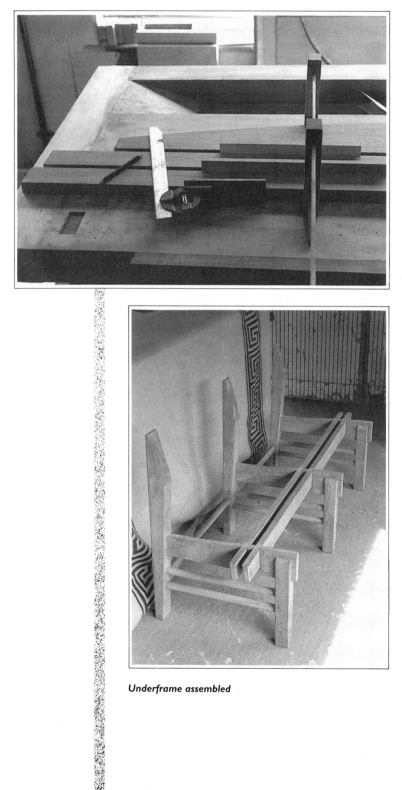

Underframe assembled

Back rails, cramped together, being marked for length

Assuming the use of two rails, however, the space between them is determined by the thickness of the arm support, and I should emphasise here that thicknesses given are the minimum advisable for strength and stability. When cutting the halvings be careful of the short grain between the joints – it is rather vulnerable until the joint is finally assembled. During the assembly I would recommend knocking the two front rails down on to the seat rail halvings together so that the short grain is equally supported from both ends.

The lower rails are round in section and can be produced by turning, though expect a degree of whip in producing the longer lengths. Alternatively they can be produced by routing followed by careful hand finishing. The side rails relative to the back rails are offset to allow maximum depth of joint. The joint itself is left barefaced and can be pinned using 6mm dowel.

The back support slats are simply screwed to the back legs. They should be prepared a little over length and the top piece shaped. A piece of flexible material, like plywood, can be used to spring the curve – you'll need a friend to help mark it out.

Having drilled the clearance holes for the screws and counterbored for the plugs, cramp the three slats on to the back legs with scraps of 9mm ply as spacers. When they are positioned correctly mark pilot holes on the back legs. Mark the angled ends across the whole assembly.

The arm and its supporting structure are to some extent a conceit. They do not contribute structurally to the design, but they do add a great deal to the overall visual composition. They are intended as repositories for soothing libations – preferably of the long and cold variety – and emphatically not for the backsides of the assembled company. Sit on them at your peril.

The lower part of the support, as already mentioned, is screwed or bolted to the front rails. The top end of the arm supports are tenoned into the underside of the arm itself. This joint could equally well be effected using threaded inserts in the support and bolting from the topside of the arm. Threaded inserts are basically a tube with a coarse thread on the outside, a fine thread on the inside (most commonly M6) to take a suitable bolt. They are extremely useful and versatile and are generally available from a variety of fittings suppliers. However, if the top end of the arm supports are tenoned the shoulders should be angled but the stub tenon is square to the face of the arm.

The back of the arm is fixed to the side of the back leg by a turned connector. This can be fixed barefaced into the leg, but requires a shoulder and a 10mm spigot turned down to go into the edge of the arm. The assembly of this awkward corner begins with the lower front supports while the arm is first fixed to the back leg then pivoted down on to the tenons. Because of the angles involved, bringing pressure to bear on the tenons is awkward and is most easily effected with a deep-throated speed cramp and a suitably angled cramping block.

Arm assembly

ASSEMBLY

For the sake of clarity the overall order of assembly should run as:

1 Front legs to back legs.
2 Back and front rails followed by back support slats.
3 Arm assembly.
4 Finally the seat slats. These are screwed and plugged to the seat rails and notched round the arm supports. They are spaced 12mm apart and the front edge of the front slat should be softened by a chamfer or radius.

CUTTING LIST

Finished sizes (mm)

Back legs	(3)	710 x 60 x 60
Front legs	(3)	340 x 60 x 45
Seat rails	(3)	530 x 100 x 20
Long rails	(2)	1540 x 70 x 20
Turned rails	(6)	480 x 25
Turned rails	(2)	650 x 25
Arms	(2)	490 x 120 x 20
Arm supports	(4)	230 x 30 x 22
Back slats	(2)	1450 x 50 x 20
Back slats	(1)	1480 x 125 x 20
Seat slats	(8)	1640 x 50 x 20

PAIR OF TABLES

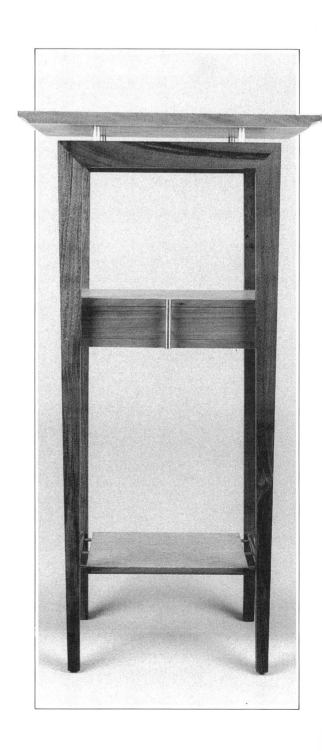

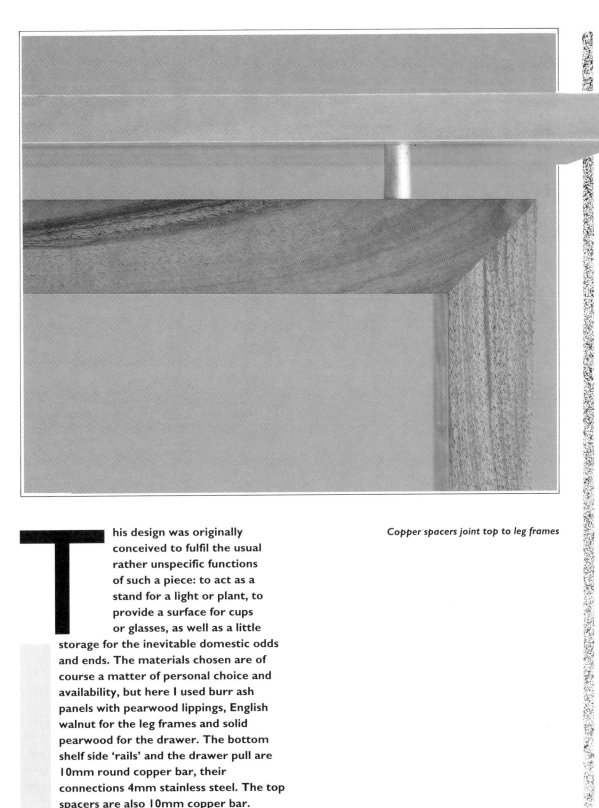

Copper spacers joint top to leg frames

T his design was originally conceived to fulfil the usual rather unspecific functions of such a piece: to act as a stand for a light or plant, to provide a surface for cups or glasses, as well as a little storage for the inevitable domestic odds and ends. The materials chosen are of course a matter of personal choice and availability, but here I used burr ash panels with pearwood lippings, English walnut for the leg frames and solid pearwood for the drawer. The bottom shelf side 'rails' and the drawer pull are 10mm round copper bar, their connections 4mm stainless steel. The top spacers are also 10mm copper bar.

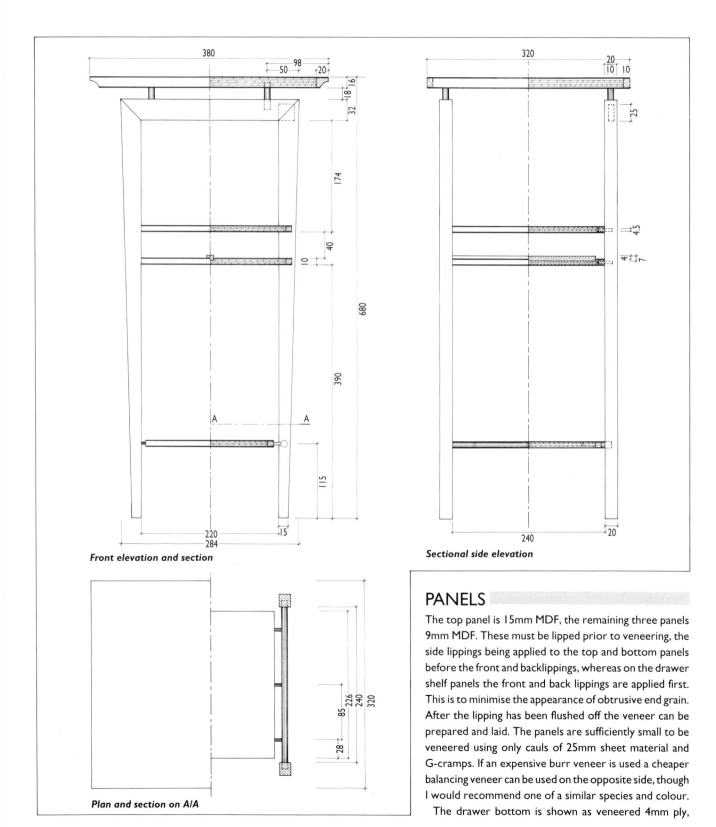

Front elevation and section

Sectional side elevation

Plan and section on A/A

PANELS

The top panel is 15mm MDF, the remaining three panels 9mm MDF. These must be lipped prior to veneering, the side lippings being applied to the top and bottom panels before the front and backlippings, whereas on the drawer shelf panels the front and back lippings are applied first. This is to minimise the appearance of obtrusive end grain. After the lipping has been flushed off the veneer can be prepared and laid. The panels are sufficiently small to be veneered using only cauls of 25mm sheet material and G-cramps. If an expensive burr veneer is used a cheaper balancing veneer can be used on the opposite side, though I would recommend one of a similar species and colour.

The drawer bottom is shown as veneered 4mm ply,

though veneer may not be thought essential. The top panel is eventually moulded on two sides only, using a 30mm-diameter cove cutter preferably with the router mounted in a table. The lower drawer panel has a 12mm wide, 3mm deep, routed groove running centrally from the back edge, stopped 14mm from the front edge, to take the drawer guide.

LEG FRAMES

The front and back frames are square and parallel on the inside, the legs tapering from top (32mm wide) to the bottom (15mm wide) on the outside edges. Careful assembly is required if accuracy is to be maintained. The top joint is mitred and reinforced with a loose tenon of 9mm ply. If any flushing-off of the joint is required, do as much as possible before gluing up. This is because the individual frames are not very strong until the panels are jointed to them.

PANEL/FRAME CONSTRUCTION

The top is jointed to the top edge of the leg frames by means of copper spacers. These have no shoulder but are let barefaced into pre-drilled holes. Where a metal component is jointed to either metal or wood, epoxy glue is used in every case, after thorough degreasing of the metal.

The drawer panels are jointed to the frames using 4.5mm (3/16") dowels. When marking out for drilling the frames be sure to use the inside (parallel) edge as the datum, not the tapering outside edge. A simple drilling guide with tacked-on stops is an invaluable aid to accuracy when drilling here, and though this takes a little time, will actually save marking out each centre individually. To help ensure the top and bottom drawer shelves are parallel, cramp the front and back leg frames together and transfer drilling centres with try-square rather than relying solely on measurement.

The bottom shelf side rails are let barefaced into the leg frames. The drilling of the copper itself is best entrusted to an engineer with appropriate equipment as the soft metal very quickly work-hardens when drilled at wood-working speeds. It is possible, though, to achieve the desired result with the bar cramped into either a V-block or cradle (both can be improvised quickly from wood or sheet material). When drilling this component it is of course essential that the bar be prevented from twisting when being moved laterally, or the stainless steel

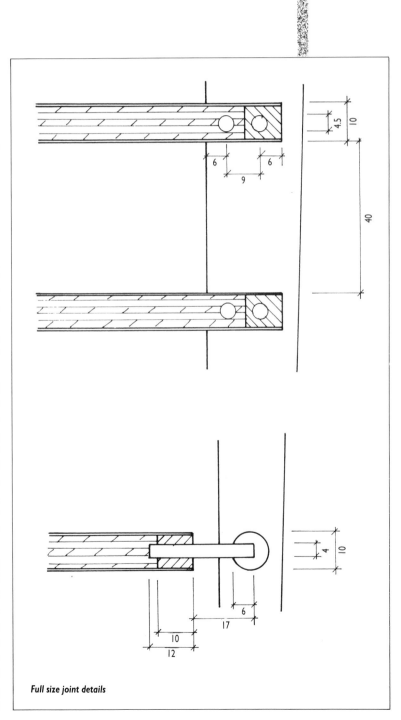

Full size joint details

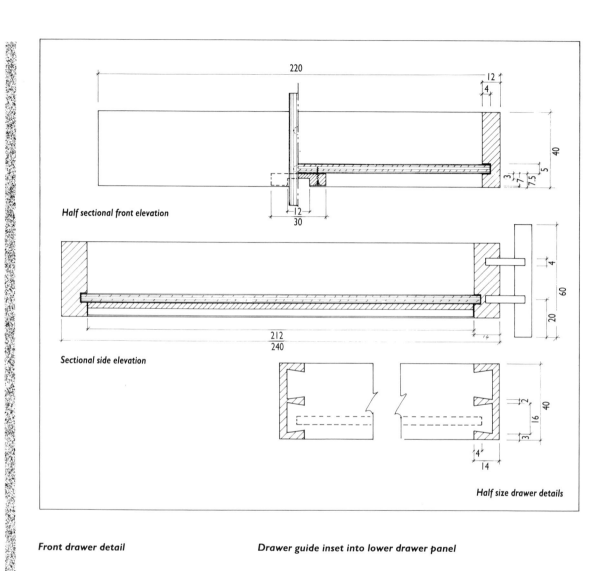

220

12

4

40

Half sectional front elevation

3
7
7.5
5

12
30

Sectional side elevation

4

60

20

212
240

Half size drawer details

2
16
40
3

4
14

Front drawer detail

Drawer guide inset into lower drawer panel

connectors will be out of alignment. Due to direction of entry the bottom shelf should be assembled to the side rails before assembling this, and the drawer shelves to the leg frames. As far as possible use light cramps to avoid distorting the framework. When this process is complete the top can be fixed.

The drawer is unconventional in that the sides are visible at all times and the front and back are symmetrical, except for the notch at the back which allows the passage of the guide. The guide (mounted in the top side of the lower drawer shelf) is located in a grooved runner fitted between the drawer front and back, and glued and/or screwed to the drawer bottom.

The dimensions of the drawer should be taken from the surrounding framework in the usual way, the dovetails cut and the bottom glued in. The drawer should be fitted so that the sides do not touch the front frame when it is moved in and out, the only points of contact being the edges of the drawer sides and the guide within the runner.

Both back and sides need to be polished in a manner appropriate to the finish used elsewhere on the table. With the materials used in the original, oil was used on the walnut and pre-catalysed cellulose lacquer elsewhere.

The pair of tables

CUTTING LIST

Finished sizes for one table

Legs	4 x 646 x 32 x 20	Walnut
Rails	2 x 284 x 32 x 20	Walnut
Top lippings	2 x 300 x 20 x 16	Pear
	2 x 284 x 32 x 20	Pear
Mid panel lippings	4 x 244 x 10 x 10	Pear
	4 x 240 x 10 x 10	Pear
Lower shelf lippings	2 x 204 x 10 x 10	Pear
	2 x 228 x 10 x 10	Pear
Drawer runner	1 x 224 x 12 x 7	Pear
Drawer sides	2 x 232 x 40 x 12	Pear
Drawer front & back	2 x 220 x 40 x 12	Pear
Top	1 x 340 x 300 x 15	MDFL
Mid panels	2 x 244 x 220 x 9	MDFL
Shelf	1 x 184 x 208 x 9	MDFL
Drawer bottom	1 x 202 x 218 x 4	Plywood

Decorative veneer and backing veneer for the panels

Three feet of 3/8" round copper bar

4mm round stainless steel bar for shelf spacers

CD STORAGE
SHELVING

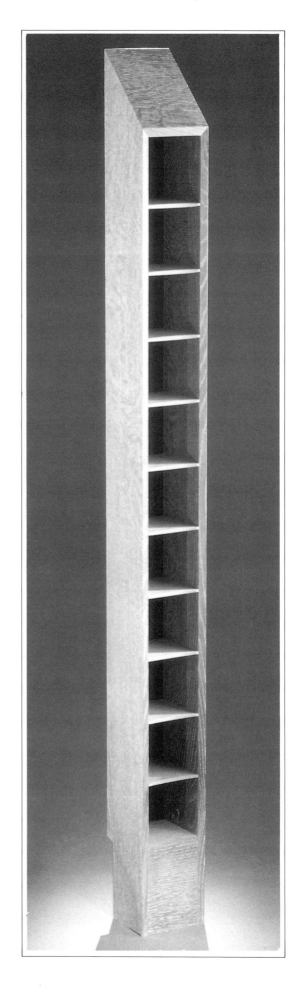

Shelving as a whole rarely provokes a great deal of aesthetic or emotional interest compared to other branches of furniture making. At one extreme, the wealthy literati or collector might install a built-in library (almost always using eighteenth and nineteenth century patterns, it would seem), while on the other hand, the cheaper and quicker an approximately horizontal surface can be thrown up and forgotten about, the better. Putting up a shelf has become a sub-handyman activity, which, though there may be all sorts of legitimate reasons for this, is a pity. Shelving of even the simplest kind can make as great a contribution to a room as any well-conceived, well-executed piece of furniture. While the two main items described here are relatively sophisticated projects, even the poorly equipped novice woodworker is capable of considerably enhancing his or her home using very simple techniques and easily accessible materials.

It's worth mentioning here that solid timber, particularly halfway decent hardwood, is far stiffer than that convenient but soulless material, melamine-faced chipboard, so quite apart from any aesthetic qualities, wooden shelves are not nearly so liable to the terminal droop which so often characterises inadequately supported man-made board.

I have made a number of wall mounted shelves for kitchen, bathroom and bedroom to accommodate those endless jars and bottles that clutter all our lives, based on nothing more than a halving-cum-housing joint, which provides surprising cantilever strength. This is admittedly appropriate only to relatively narrow shelves, being really just a beefed-up spice rack, but the idea can obviously be extended and strengthened by using corner blocks or simple brackets to further support the shelves.

In order to avoid the use of steel or aluminium track systems for bookshelves, I have often made up triangular wooden brackets and wall mounted these by means of keyhole slots routed in the back edge which engage on to the heads of countersunk screws driven into the wall. The bracket just fits over the screw heads and drops down.

This system has enormous strength, even on stud walls (provided appropriate wall plugs are used), and has the advantage of leaving no fixings visible. Of course the bracket itself can be shaped and detailed in any way appropriate to the situation. Its primary purpose is to transfer the load from the outer edge of the shelf to lower down the vertical plane of the wall, and while a triangle is the most logical form for this to take, it can be curved or carved or drilled or whatever, as fancy dictates.

Freestanding shelving brings us nearer to what is commonly perceived as furniture proper. I don't want to concern myself yet with case furniture which can involve sophisticated cabinetmaking skills, but again I just wish to emphasise that it is possible to make substantial and satisfying objects with only the judicious application of simple jointing and fixing techniques.

I would suggest that bookshelves are generally best made with solid ends, at least where large numbers of books need storing. Where this is the case, bear in mind that the accumulated weight of hundreds of books is enormous and requires careful consideration of both structure and materials. Where well-executed traditional jointing – housings and mortise and tenons – is used to fix shelf to ends, adequate stiffness can usually be achieved without recourse to bracing frames or back panels. Where adjustable shelving is required, some form of bracing will almost certainly be necessary, and a back panel grooved or rebated in is merely the simplest way of effecting this.

DISPLAY SHELVING

Display shelving prompts a different response altogether, though much depends on the formality and preciousness or otherwise of the objects on show. Solid ends can work very well, and by enclosing and 'framing', attention can be focused on the display, but they do to some extent restrict vision; it thus makes sense to use open frameworks to allow greater visual access to the objects on show, and also results in an object which is in itself less bulky and less intrusive on the space of the room.

Possibly the most direct method of erecting this type of shelving is to screw uprights to the edge of the shelves. This is a technical and conceptual advance on using piles of bricks as supports, but only by a narrow margin, whereas straightforward notched joints and edge halvings provide excellent support and bracing, and, as an added bonus, such expressed jointing will often result in unpretentious but satisfying decorative detail.

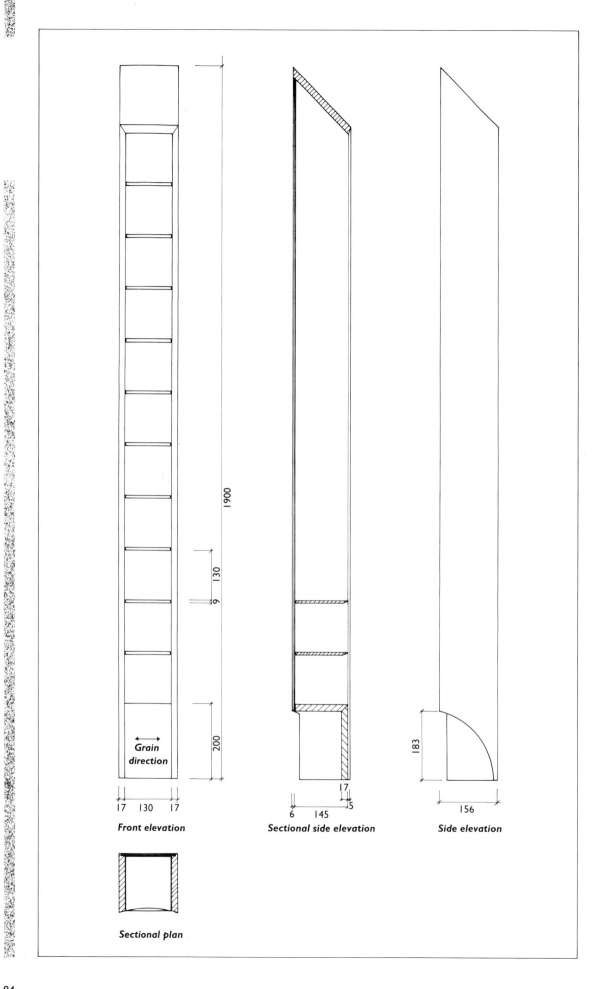

Grain direction

1900

130

9

200

17 130 17

Front elevation

17

6 145 5

Sectional side elevation

183

156

Side elevation

Sectional plan

Using different timbers for uprights and shelves respectively will reduce the monolithic quality of the unit, though this quality might in some circumstances be desirable.

I should make it clear that this is not in any sense an attempt to make rules or lay down laws. The objective is only to make tentative suggestions as to a very few of the possibilities, and by thinking for a moment extend, maybe even enhance what might be done otherwise. But enough of this: onwards and – maybe – upwards.

CD STORAGE

The intention behind this piece is to provide a solution to what is these days a common enough problem – the storage of electronic software in one form or another, and to invest the resulting object with what I like to call 'presence' without ignoring the practical requirement. The basic concept is capable of considerable dimensional 'tweaking' to accommodate storage needs apart from compact discs, but as it stands will accommodate over 100 CD units.

In order to contrast with – indeed to gain relief from – the super-regular, shiny plastic cases of the CDs, I used a solid timber, in this case brushed, fumed and limed oak, but the construction will work using sheet materials. The combination of colour and surface texture achieved by the wire brushing, fuming etc. which I have used extensively in the last few years is certainly time-consuming, but adds immeasurably to the material quality. The colour is sombre but not dull or oppressive – the chemical reaction doesn't deny the timber anything in the way that conventional staining does, while the open-grained texture produced by the brushing emphasises the toughness and organic quality of the timber. It's not too effete, it's not too violent, and it sure is woody.

The shelves are sycamore to provide contrast, and the front edges carry one of the major details of the piece. While this bevel and curve is nothing if not reticent, it considerably enriches the overall effect by reducing the monotonous rhythm of the shelves. It also has a practical benefit in that it allows fingertip access to the bottom edge of the CD cases, facilitating their withdrawal if tightly packed.

The carcase construction begins with the angled top mitred to the sides. When preparing the top allow extra width to accommodate the cleaning up of the back and front edges, as shown in the drawing. The front edge of the top and the corresponding edges of the sides are

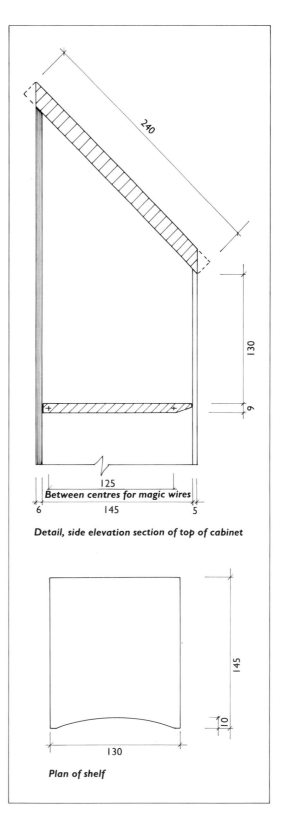

Detail, side elevation section of top of cabinet

Plan of shelf

Sides and base ready for assembly

bevelled back 5mm to line up with the front panel of the base unit. The mitre is cut after the three pieces have been precisely dimensioned to width and thickness. I have the luxury of a panel saw with mitre fence and tilting arbor, but the dimensions here allow the joint to be quite easily shot by hand.

The mitre needs a locating and reinforcing joint such as a biscuit or loose tongue and groove, and this is worked within 2 or 3mm of the inside of the mitre (i.e. where the material is thickest) to minimise the short grain problem. The joint can also be reinforced and decorated using pins or dowels similar to the nesting table stool design (q.v.) or veneer keys.

The bottom shelf is mitred to a fascia panel to form a kind of internal plinth. This L-shaped piece is then biscuited or dowelled to the sides. In solid timber the grain direction of the fascia panel may cause movement problems if glued across its entire width, so, erring on the side of caution, I only glued the fascia panel joint halfway down and fixed the bottom with a shrinkage plate, thus allowing the timber to shrink and expand without the risk of breaking the joint or splitting the wood.

The other major structural element, which is especially important in correcting bowed sides, is the back panel. As this is a wall fixed piece, and the individual compartments are small and quite shadowy, the material of the back does not make a huge decorative impact. It is hardly worthwhile therefore going to the expense and trouble of using even a veneered panel, let alone a framed solid timber back.

In this instance we used painted 6mm MDF, rebated into the sides and screwed. The rebate does not extend across the back edge of the top because of the difficulty of working the correct angle there – not impossible with the right equipment, but more trouble than it's worth – rather, the top of the back panel is bevelled to butt up to the inside of the sloping top. Stop the side panel rebates in line with the bottom edge of the top or you will end up with little triangular 'ears' needing to be filled up. A countersunk clearance hole to take the wall fixing screw should be drilled at any convenient height, but preferably behind the position of one of the shelves.

The shelves are mounted on magic wire supports, which are simple to fix and invisible when fitted; the drilling for these must be done prior to assembly. Cramp the sides together when marking these out to ensure consistent accuracy.

The last job before starting the assembly process is to rout the curved recess at the foot of the sides. The recess is only 5mm deep and the curve is best routed from a hardboard template, which should have the concave curve worked on it, allowing it to be held to the sides over a greater area than if convex. Start the routing from the back corner and work towards the curved shoulder, taking care to keep the router, which will only be supported on half its base, upright. Any unevenness can be planed, scraped and sanded clean. As the unit will be fixed to the wall, the back edge is cut away to fit over a skirting board. This recess coincides with the line of the curve.

We are now ready for dry test assembly. It's not essential to have all the shelves routed for the magic wires, but it is helpful to have them ready in order to check alignment, as if there is any problem in this respect, it will very difficult to correct after gluing up. All the cleaning up of the front edge bevels at the top should also

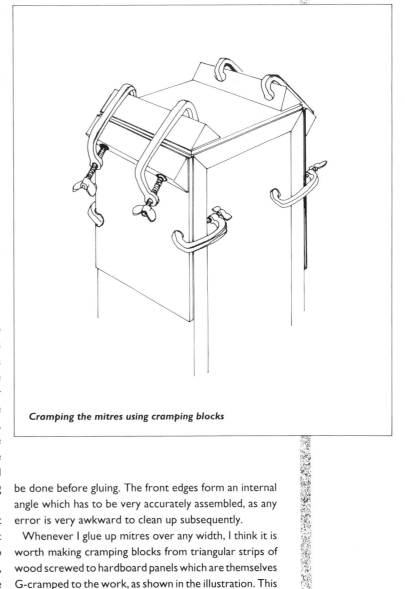

Cramping the mitres using cramping blocks

be done before gluing. The front edges form an internal angle which has to be very accurately assembled, as any error is very awkward to clean up subsequently.

Whenever I glue up mitres over any width, I think it is worth making cramping blocks from triangular strips of wood screwed to hardboard panels which are themselves G-cramped to the work, as shown in the illustration. This provides the most direct pressure on the mitre joint,

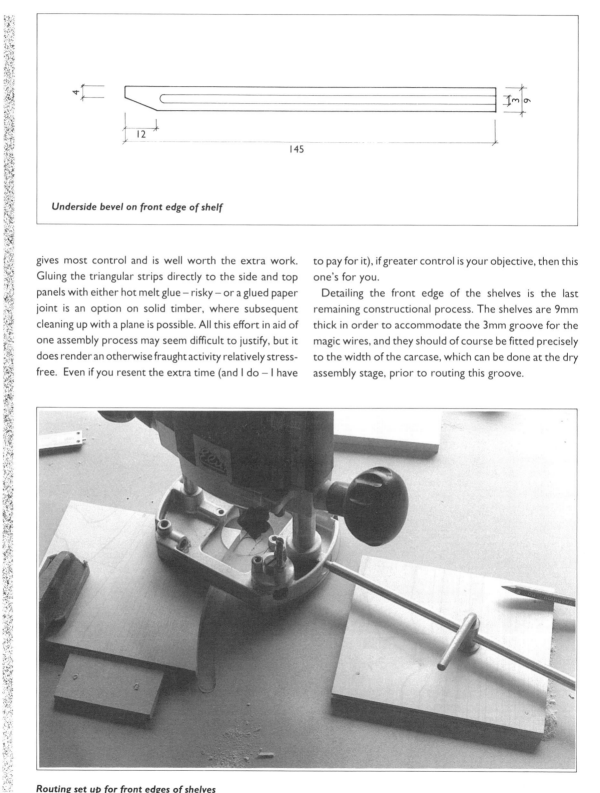

4

12

145

3

9

Underside bevel on front edge of shelf

gives most control and is well worth the extra work. Gluing the triangular strips directly to the side and top panels with either hot melt glue – risky – or a glued paper joint is an option on solid timber, where subsequent cleaning up with a plane is possible. All this effort in aid of one assembly process may seem difficult to justify, but it does render an otherwise fraught activity relatively stress-free. Even if you resent the extra time (and I do – I have to pay for it), if greater control is your objective, then this one's for you.

Detailing the front edge of the shelves is the last remaining constructional process. The shelves are 9mm thick in order to accommodate the 3mm groove for the magic wires, and they should of course be fitted precisely to the width of the carcase, which can be done at the dry assembly stage, prior to routing this groove.

Routing set up for front edges of shelves

The front edge is then bevelled on the underside, 4mm in the thickness and 12mm back as in the illustration. This can be routed or spindled if you have appropriate cutters, or planed. The curve is then routed using a trammel bar fixed to the router. For the sake of consistency it's worth fixing some stops to hold the shelf on to a base plate – scrap MDF or chipboard will do – and also pinning a piece of timber the same thickness as the shelf to provide a centre for the trammel, and to keep the router level. A trial set up of this jig is shown in the photograph. If no trammel bar is at hand (though they are easily improvised from strips of timber or sheet material), the curve can be routed from a hardboard template, or even spokeshaved if you prefer. The effect of the curve combined with bevel is to reduce the apparent thickness of the shelves at either side, a simple means of giving a visual lift.

FINISHING

The finishing processes will depend on the materials used: in this case the oak was first brushed with as large a rotary wire brush as could be obtained. This does more than open up the grain – it actually erodes the softer grain and distresses the surface, and any resulting splintery edges will need sanding and chamfering afterwards. For fuming, it is necessary to construct some sort of box or tent from chipboard and/or a polythene sheet. I have often draped plastic sheeting over trestles and taped the edges to the floor, without needing to use great finesse. Industrial strength ammonia (.880 solution) requires careful handling, however; if it gets into your eyes or lungs it hurts. A lot.

Get everything ready beforehand – the cabinet carcase in the box or tent, with only sufficient access for a couple of jars containing the ammonia. You won't need a great deal of the ammonia itself; about 20mm in the bottom of a jam jar should be plenty. Pour the solution into the jars as close to the fuming tent as practicable – *don't* run around the workshop clutching containers of noxious fluid – and seal the tent as quickly as possible. Goggles and masks are a sensible safety precaution, particularly against splashes in the eyes, and reduce general unpleasantness.

I usually leave the fuming process to work overnight or over a weekend at most, by which time all the colour change that is going to occur will have taken place. On opening the tent, make sure the workshop is well ventilated for obvious reasons. I usually then put fumed work aside, or even outside for a day or two, if conditions permit, to let the smell wear off.

Fumed oak in itself is in my view extraordinarily dull and depressing, but liming it achieves a uniquely soft grey-brown effect. This can be done either with liming wax on its own or with liming paste, which is then sealed with laquer; in both cases the wax or paste is generously applied and then removed with white spirit-soaked rags followed by dry buffing. When sealing liming paste, it is as well to prepare a test piece to make sure the lacquer will adhere. Leave the paste to thoroughly dry after buffing, whatever laquer is chosen, though I have found waterborne laquer, which can be sprayed or brushed on, to be very successful in this as in other applications.

CUTTING LIST

Finished sizes

Sides	2 x 1900 x 156 x 17	Oak
Top	1 x 164 x 240 x 17	Oak
Base (front)	1 x 130 x 200 x 17	Oak
(shelf)	1 x 130 x 145 x 17	Oak
Shelves	10 x 130 x 145 x 9	Sycamore
Back	1 x 1685 x 154 x 6	MDF

ALCOVE SHELVING

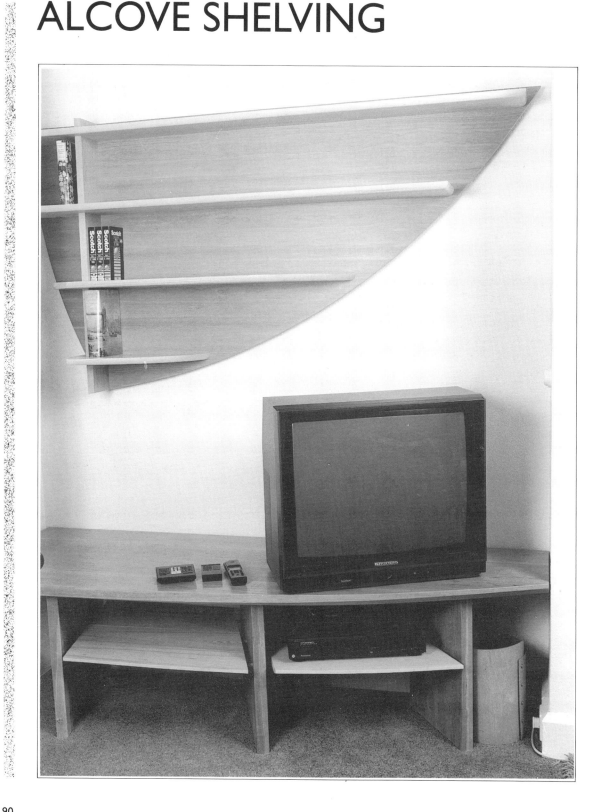

Before proceeding with this project I feel I should offer a number of qualifications. Firstly, the title might be slightly misleading in that the design does not use an alcove as part of the structure, but does occupy the space in a deliberate and precise way. Secondly, the lower part of the unit (the TV and video stand), while incorporating shelving, is in fact more akin to a low table. While I shall indicate the construction of this in general terms, the principles of the jointing and assembly techniques are similar to those used in the desk project (q.v.). Lastly, I suspect it unlikely in the extreme that the particular conditions that produced this design solution will apply in many other instances. In which case, yet again I would urge you not to view the project as an inflexible master plan but to take the ideas and rework them according to your own needs.

This is obviously not a project for the inexperienced maker (though the wall hung shelving does not represent too great a challenge), and it should not be beyond your ability, enthusiasm or commitment to adjust dimensions, details and construction without entirely forsaking the spirit of the piece. Were the same commission to be repeated, I would certainly make changes myself: not that I view what has been made as flawed, but no conception is immaculate, and there are always different ways of doing things. So don't rely on being spoonfed by me, and don't be afraid to implement your own imagination.

The practical essence of the brief was to use a corner alcove to provide storage for a large TV and associated paraphernalia, as well as shelves for tapes and the usual domestic bric-a-brac. The position of the television was more or less fixed, and its looming presence on an existing stand made for a lot of dead space around it. My first objective was to use that space more effectively and to re-occupy it more expressively.

The curved plan was suggested by the simplest constraints : at one end a window board on the return wall determined the maximum possible width of the television shelf, narrowing at the other end to the depth of the chimney breast which formed the alcove. The television itself needed to be angled in order to be seen from every part of the room, and while a wedge-shaped plan would have been sufficient to accommodate this, the curve appears, and is, more generous. The 'bite' from the wider end is specific only to this room, in that it forms a space for the drawn, full length curtains.

Having established this, the whole scheme became an interplay between straight lines and curves, the latter being enlivened by deep and, in some cases, twisting chamfers. One important effect of this organisation of the plan is that the unit 'offers' itself out of the corner, facilitating access to the stored objects, rather than stolidly sitting there, pushed back into it.

The next major decision was to break the structural connection between the shelving and the lower unit. This was mainly to offset the sheer bulk of the television; had it been contained within a conventional rack of shelves, it would have overwhelmed everything.

Wall hanging the shelves from a panel prompted the curved edge which relates to the lower unit and has a clear logic in sweeping up behind the TV, where no storage would be possible. The formal presence of the shelving now stands up to that of the TV and balances it. All of this lends some credence to the view that awkward

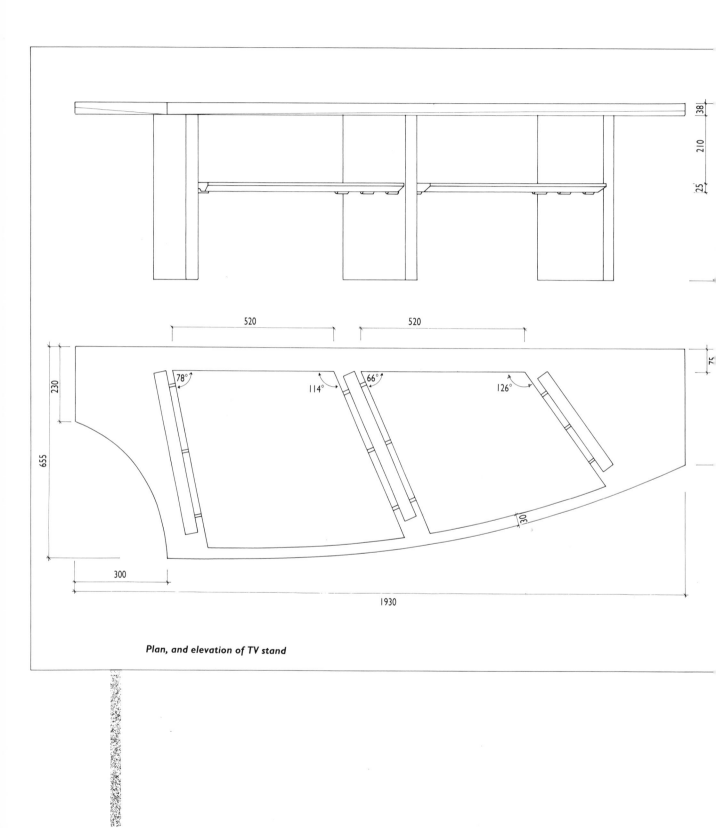

Plan, and elevation of TV stand

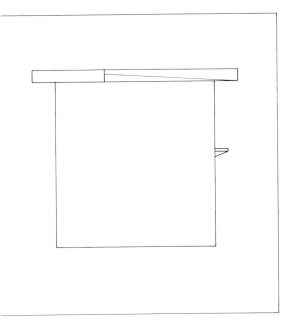

Mortise/housing joint

problems – like what can you do with enormous TV sets? – can lead to unexpectedly satisfying design solutions.

MAKING THE TV STAND

All components are solid timber, biscuit jointed in the usual way. Be careful to place the biscuits in positions where they will not subsequently be exposed when the curves are cut. The legs are different widths, and on plan they are: (left) 510mm, (middle) 490mm, (right) 355mm. As shown in the drawing, they are set in from the back edge of the top by 75mm, but each is at a different angle to that edge. These angles must be carefully set out on the underside of the prepared top.

Each leg joint consists of three 30mm square x 30mm deep tenons across the width with a 10mm deep housing between, as in the photograph. The mortises and negative side of the housing are routed against a cramped batten, while the tenons are routed and sawn. These joints, well fitted, provide complete solidity. One advantage of the legs not being parallel is the consequent reduction in the likelihood of racking, and no further bracing is necessary.

When these joints have been fitted, the shaping of the top and the front edges can be completed. The curves are sawn by bandsaw or jigsaw and cleaned up with a router against a template or by hand. The exact nature of the chamfering and degree of twist on these edges is a matter of personal preference. The diminishing bevels, which appear as twists, are worked with a spokeshave.

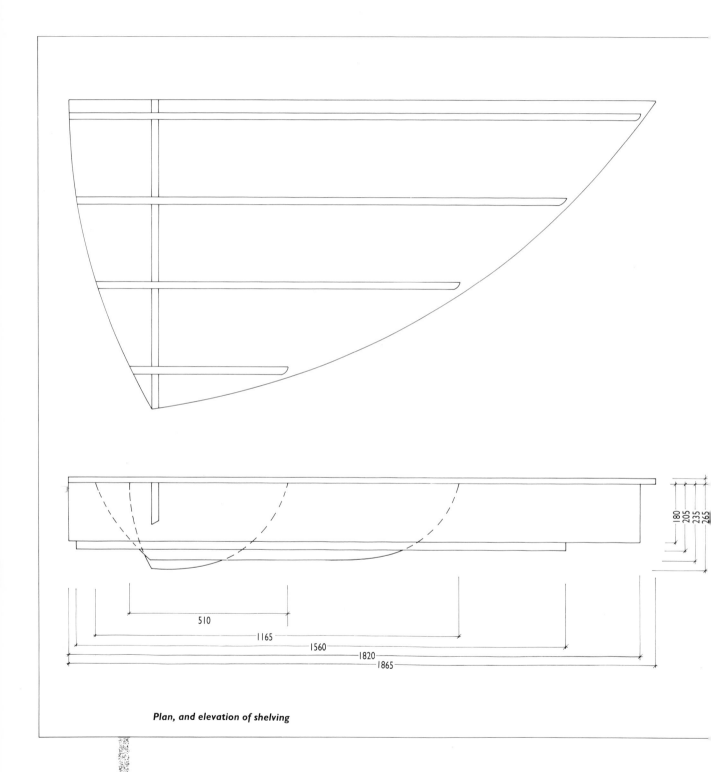

Plan, and elevation of shelving

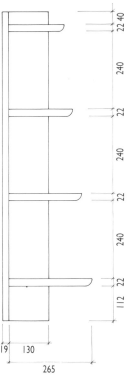

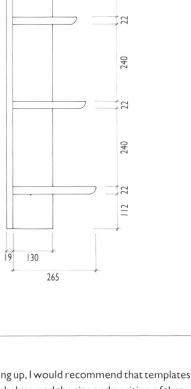

Preliminary assembly showing shelf templates

Cramping up

Before gluing up, I would recommend that templates are made of the shelves, and the size and position of these can then be checked before any irreversible steps are taken. Unless you possess deep-throated cramps of a suitable length, pressure will depend on using substantial and slightly curved cramping blocks, as shown in the photograph. In order to avoid much wailing and gnashing of the teeth, get a friend to help hold blocks and cramps. Pressure should be applied evenly from each side and, while the position of the leg cannot move and the shoulder line should take care of itself (you've already checked during a dry run), do make sure that the legs are exactly square to the top. Small adjustments to the cramps make a crucial difference here.

One small discussion arises here: that of whether or not to prefinish areas that will be difficult to get at after assembly. I would certainly recommend sanding to a

Detail of shelf supports

finish level on the legs and underside of the top, regardless of what polish is used. If lacquering, as opposed to oiling or waxing, I believe there is some justification for prefinishing in order to avoid the problems of spraying and cutting back into internal corners. The problems are, firstly, patience – one naturally wants to get on and assemble a piece; secondly, all joints need to be masked; and lastly, extreme care and neatness in gluing up is then essential. One cannot legislate for every situation, but in each case weigh up the pros and cons before making an educated decision.

THE VIDEO SHELVING

The shelves for the video, satellite box or whatever are next on the agenda. Because of their asymmetrical shape some waste from a solid wood panel is inevitable, and you should allow for this at the preparation stage, consulting the cutting list. The visual impact of the grain is not great,

as the shelves are tucked under the top, but the front edge protrudes beyond the fronts of the legs, so it's worth taking care here. In practice it makes little difference whether the grain is parallel to the back edge or front: if it is parallel to the front, the grain follows and emphasises the curve of the top slightly more.

The shaping of the two panels is only a matter of careful marking out, using the back edge as the reference edge when measuring the angles. As mentioned above, hardboard templates are well worth making as checks. Though there are many types of proprietary shelf supports available, I wanted a large gap at each end of the shelf for ventilation. This isn't essential of course, and certainly the size of the gap is not critical, but the visual separation also contributes to the overall effect.

The supports are 12.7mm (½") turned ash pegs which locate in a half round routed groove on the underside of the shelf, as shown in the photograph. The drilling in the legs is more easily done before gluing up, but access is not difficult afterwards. The marking out for the grooves needs to be very accurate, or a sloppy, rocking shelf will result. It is best to mark the centres on the legs and then offer the prepared shelf panels up to these and transfer them, rather than relying on measurement alone.

The back edges of the shelf line up with the rearmost corners of the back legs, so use this as a datum. One simple way to do this would be to rest the whole assembly on the back edges of the legs on the bench, with the top overhanging. The shelves can then be inserted, supported on their back edges and the marks transferred. The length of the half round groove is not critical, but should be consistent. It will need to be routed from a fence – a small piece of MDF will do – cramped to the shelf, square to the edge. Finally, the bevelled edges can be planed or spokeshaved.

THE WALL HUNG SHELVING

This is an extension, albeit a fairly large one of the 'beefed-up spice rack' kind of shelving mentioned in the last chapter: if that was beefed up, perhaps this one's been taking steroids! Seriously though, the basic principles are exactly the same, but in this instance the back panel not only enables the piece to be wall mounted but supports the shelves themselves. (The shelves as shown in the drawing were only required for relatively light objects and for storing nothing taller than a video tape, and while they are extremely strong, I would reinforce them further for constant heavier weights.)

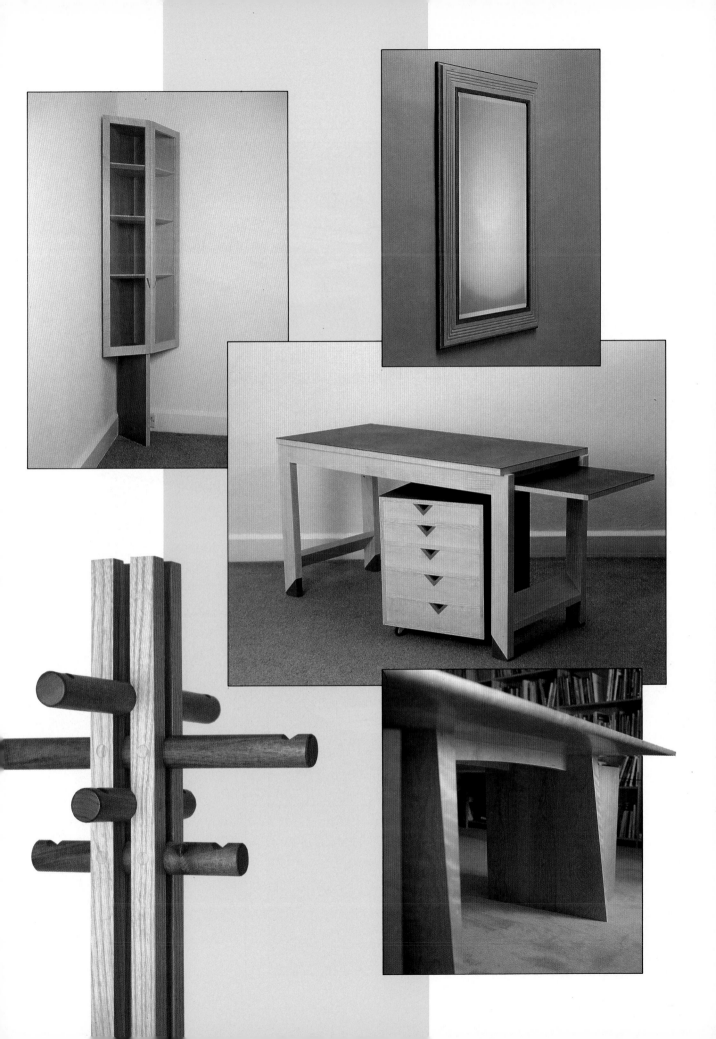

The curved edges are marked out by plotting five or six points then springing a strip of timber or ply to connect these points. The curves are sawn and can be cleaned up by hand or routed from a template. It is important to keep these edges consistently square or the lipping glue line will suffer.

The back panel is veneered MDF. The lipping can be applied before or after veneering, and consists of 4mm thick solid timber. This will bend easily on to the curved edges, and masking tape will provide sufficient 'cramping' pressure when gluing.

Unless you happen to have a large veneer press in your workshop, this part of the job will have to be put out to a veneerer – hammer veneering with scotch glue is an option I prefer not to think about. Alternatives are preveneered board, which is now becoming more generally available in a fair variety of timbers, or painted or stained ply or MDF. There are also plastic laminates on the market with real wood veneer surfaces (i.e. not grain printed paper) which are available either finished or unfinished. The advantage of these is that you will not need to either joint or press the veneer : contact adhesive provides an adequate bond.

The shelves and upright are solid wood and prepared in the usual way. The edge halving not only supplies most of the support to the shelves, but needs to be cut neatly or it will look embarrassing, as it's one of those joints – mitres are another example – where, unless the intentions are perfectly fulfilled, the failure advertises itself loudly.

The front edge of the upright is slotted to half its width to take the full thickness of the shelf (22mm). The remaining width is housed to take the same thickness to a depth of 3mm. The bulk of the waste in the slot is sawn

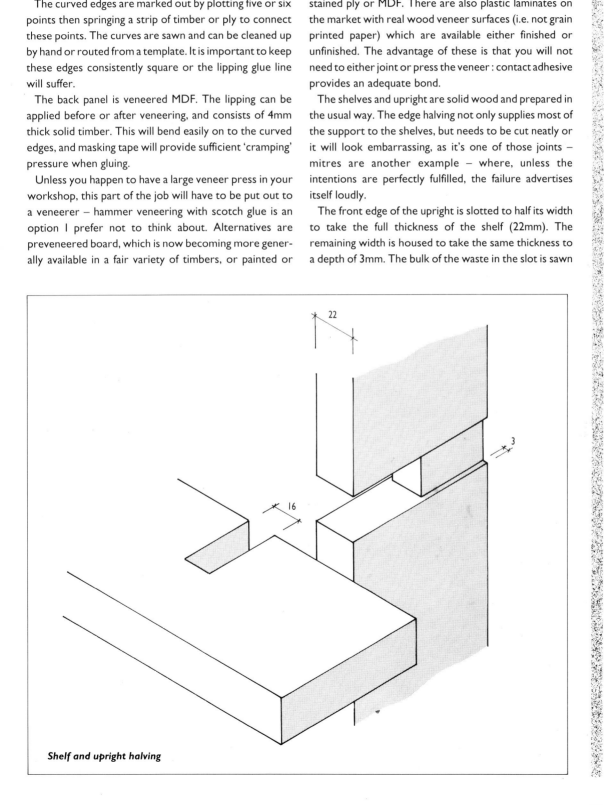

Shelf and upright halving

J

Shelving: preliminary assembly showing edge halving

away, the housing is routed and the slot cleaned up either by paring or with the router. The slot in the back edge of the shelf is worked in the same manner, but remember that it is only 16mm, the width of the housed section of the upright.

The fit should ideally require a gentle tap with a mallet: too tight, and you risk splitting the timber; but more likely, during assembly the glue can swell the joint to a surprising extent, resulting in frantic swinging of hammers, scrambling for cramps and generally unhealthy stress – both to you and the wood. The halvings should be tried home dry, and when knocking apart, take special care not to skew the shelf in the joint, which will encourage splitting. The length and the curved ends of the shelves are determined by individual requirements and of course the length and shape of the back panel. The curved ends are largely a visual conceit, but do give a sculptural movement to that

area. Finally, the front edge of the upright was also bevelled, again an inessential detail, but one which works with the general orientation of the piece. The shelving is fixed to the panel by M6 machine screws which engage in threaded inserts let into the back edges of the shelves and upright. These inserts afford enormous pull-out resistance – far greater than conventional woodscrews – combined with the great strength of the bolts, and were placed at approximately 350mm centres.

After polishing, in this case two coats of waterborne lacquer sprayed on and cut back with 320 grit paper followed by wire wool, the unit is mounted by means of split battens. These need only be 13mm thick, or the gap between panel and wall will appear excessive. It is an advantage to make them fairly wide – 60mm is adequate – to increase the sheer resistance by staggering the screws. Set the battens in from the ends by at least 50mm, and mount them behind the top and third shelf down.

When fixing the battens it is helpful to have a template to check their exact alignment and parallelism as they are mounted on the wall. This is because it is impossible to see where any error might be when offering up the completed panel, which, it has to be said, is now quite heavy enough

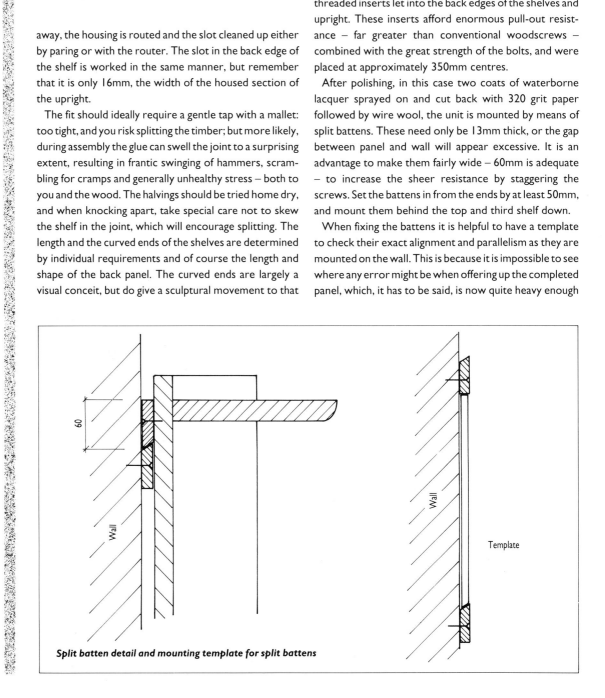

Split batten detail and mounting template for split battens

for two people to need to lift and awkward enough to handle without having to try to squint round the back. The template can be any thickness of scrap material, preferably at least 500-600mm long and sawn one edge square, with the parallel edge worked at the appropriate width and angle. The square edge then butts up against the underside of the upper wall mounted batten, giving the lower edge a positive location while marking out the lower batten, as seen in the illustration.

A final word of caution: be sure the fixings are appropriate to the type of wall before hanging something of this weight. Plaster and stud walls will obviously require expanding plugs or toggle fixings. If you're not sure which fixings to use, consult your dealer, as they say.

Detail of curved and bevelled shelf ends and uprights

CUTTING LIST

Finished sizes

TV STAND

Top	1 x 1930 x 655 x 38	Cherry
Legs	1 x 542 x 510 x 38	Cherry
	1 x 542 x 490 x 38	Cherry
	1 x 542 x 355 x 38	Cherry
Shelves	1 x 750 x 545 x 25	Ash
	1 x 775 x 500 x 25	Ash
Pegs	12 x 55 x 12.7mm diameter	

WALL HUNG SHELVING

Back panel	1 x 1865 x 960 x 19mm	Veneered MDF
Lipping	ex 5000 x 19 x 4	
Shelves	1 x 1820 x 180 x 22	Ash
	1 x 1560 x 205 x 22	Ash
	1 x 1165 x 235 x 22	Ash
	1 x 510 x 265 x 22	Ash
Upright	1 x 960 x 130 x 22	Ash
Battens	2 x 1800 x 60 x 12	Ash
	2 x 1100 x 60 x 12	Ash

LOW TABLE

This table relies for its effect on its proportion and the use of 'quiet' timber to emphasise the strong horizontal lines. Rich veneer or complex patterning would tend to overbalance the composition. In this example, partly to relate to existing pieces in the room, I used olive ash for the panels, European walnut for the legs, and copper spacers.

TOP AND LOWER SHELF

The top and lower shelf are veneered 19mm MDF and the first job is to lip these two panels. The top has a mitred lipping which requires accuracy in cutting and care when gluing. Make sure the inside dimension of the mitred lipping corresponds exactly to the length of the edge to which it is being applied. As the top is square in this instance, all four should be the same, but check anyway. An easily made shooting block, see illustration, held in the vice is a real boon when cleaning up a sawn mitre with a finely set plane. The lower shelf lippings can be butted as the leg/shelf joint conceals the end grain.

VENEERING

Due to their size, the veneering of the panels really requires a substantial press. I would not recommend relying on cauls and cramps. Professional pressing does not usually cost a great deal, particularly if you prepare the substrate and joint the veneers. One alternative would be to use pre-veneered board, which is becoming widely available in a fair variety of timbers. In this case the lipping would be exposed rather than veneered over, but this could be made a feature, particularly if a contrasting timber was used.

When veneering your own board, allow a few millimetres all round on the substrate for trimming on the saw after pressing. This I find is far easier than trimming back veneer to the substrate with all the mess of glue squeeze-out to deal with. Two points here: the width of the mitred lipping should accommodate this trimming, and when sawing across the grain of the veneer there is every likelihood of break-out, no matter how fine or sharp the saw. A positive knife line scribed across the grain will prevent this. It is worth taking this trouble even though we shall later be routing a radius on the underside of the

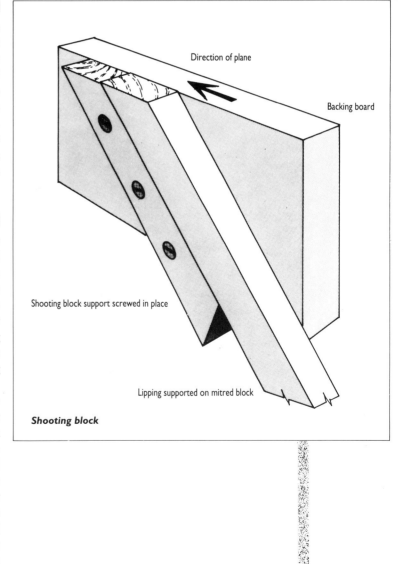

Direction of plane

Backing board

Shooting block support screwed in place

Lipping supported on mitred block

Shooting block

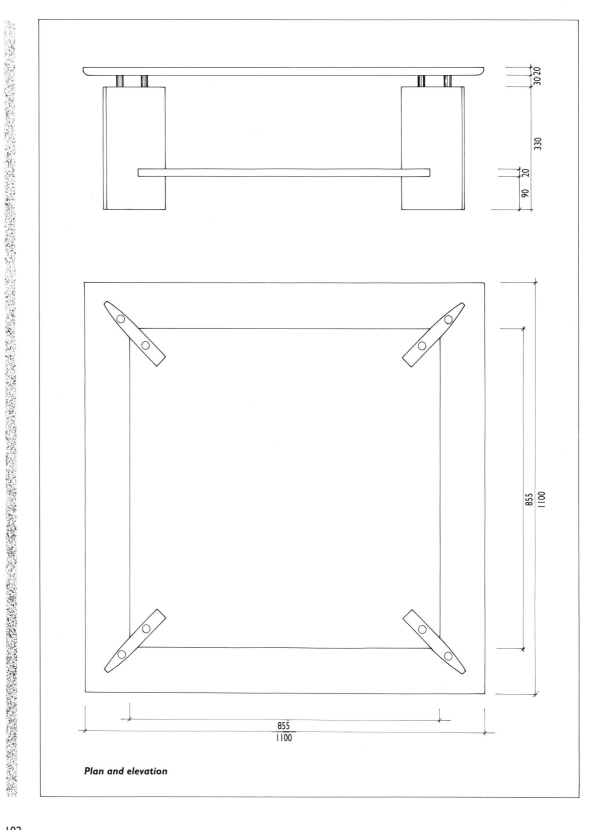

Plan and elevation

top – you never can tell how great the break-out damage might otherwise be.

Once the two panels have been made up, the leg material can be prepared and if necessary jointed to make up the required width. Do not shape the legs until the shelf and top joints have been worked.

SHELF/LEG JOINT

The shelf is jointed to the legs by a shouldered halving. A 30mm slot is sawn and/or routed into the corner of the shelf panel. The opposite side of the joint consists of a slot corresponding exactly to the thickness of the shelf panel cut into the inside edge of the leg. Rather than relying solely upon a plain cross halving, a weak joint at the best of times, the shelf slot fits into a housing (2.5mm deep each side of the leg), which continues the line of the slot in the leg. This provides a far better location and greater strength.

The housing in the leg can be routed using a cramped straight-edge as a fence or a T-square jig in conjunction with a template follower (guide bush).

After working the housing the halving can then be sawn and pared or routed.

Having trimmed the shelf panel to 855mm square, measure 25mm along from the corners (see drawing) and saw off the corners leaving a 35mm diagonal flat. The slot is sawn and/or routed through the centre line of this flat. While this can be achieved quite adequately by hand, for consistency and ease of cutting sheet material, it would be

Shelf/leg joint

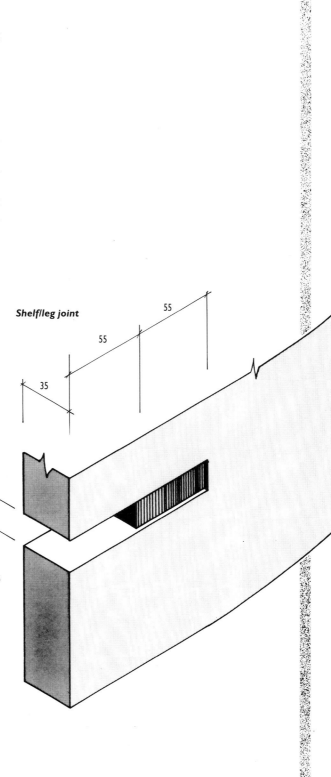

better to use the simple router jig as shown in the photograph. This is a board slotted to guide a template follower, and located by two battens screwed to the underside at 90° to each other, which centralise the jig on the corner of the panel.

The shelf slot extends 55mm in from the corner flat. The completed joint should be a push fit not requiring heavy persuasion. Concentrate on making the housing width the exact thickness of the panel. This is effectively a barefaced housing so the fit is visually critical.

SHAPING THE LEGS

The shaping of the legs comes next. The marking out of this section and the consistent centring of the drilling on the top edges is greatly assisted by the simple template shown in the photograph. Having marked the section on both top and bottom edges of the legs, most of the waste is removed with a portable power plane. This is a crude but very effective means of removing large amounts of

Leg/lower shelf joint

Routing jig for corner joint on lower shelf

material quickly. Do not expect to achieve a fine surface quality however – you will need to continue the job with handplane and abrasives.

The spacers in this example are turned ash, clad with copper tube. They are fixed into the top of the leg by means of a turned spigot and the top by means of M6 studding into a threaded insert let into the underside of the panel. It is not essential that copper, or indeed any kind of metal, be used here, but its reflective gleam does, literally, highlight the detail. The turned wood needs to be a tight fit inside the tube and is glued in with epoxy resin. First turn the wooden plug and the shoulder for the spigot. Having cut the tube fractionally over length (0.5mm) and square (use a file if necessary), glue the copper to the wood and using the existing centres (which you have sensibly not already cut off) remount the spacer on the

Template for shaped leg section and centres of threaded inserts

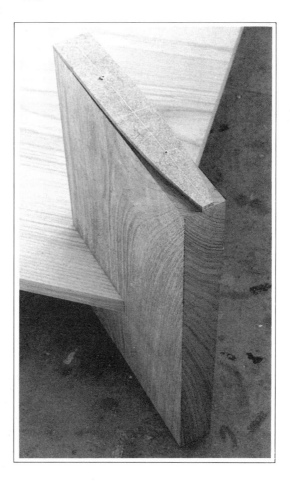

Leg plan

Centres for spigots

10

220

110

60

35

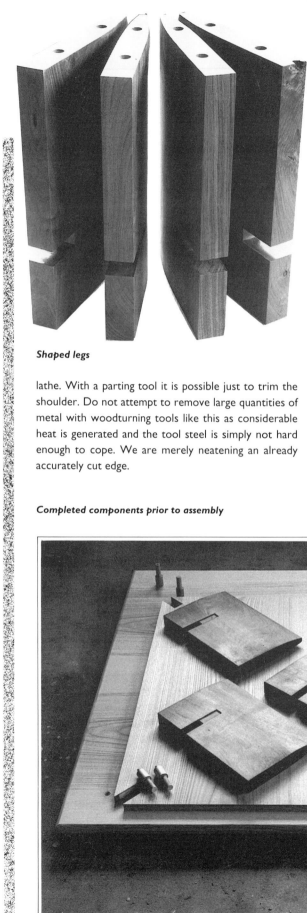

Shaped legs

lathe. With a parting tool it is possible just to trim the shoulder. Do not attempt to remove large quantities of metal with woodturning tools like this as considerable heat is generated and the tool steel is simply not hard enough to cope. We are merely neatening an already accurately cut edge.

Completed components prior to assembly

ASSEMBLY

The 40mm long spigot provides good long grain gluing into the leg. The joint to the top presents more of a problem in that the panel is only 20mm thick, which is less than adequate for a strong dowel fixing. Accordingly I used threaded inserts in the underside of the top to provide a strong fixing for the necessarily short lengths of studding. This studding (threaded steel bar bought in 1-metre lengths and cut to length) can also be fixed into the top of the spacer by means of a threaded insert. Alternatively, using M6 studding drill a 5.5mm hole, 30mm deep, in the spacer, slot the end of the studding with a hacksaw to provide a drive, and then epoxy glue the studding in. It cuts its own thread in the timber, and even in end grain (theoretically bad practice) makes a strong connection.

The centres for the inserts into the top must be carefully marked using the aforementioned template, which should ensure consistency between the centres. The template is positioned along a diagonal drawn from each corner, the two centres being respectively 140mm and 240mm in from the corner. The spacers are dry-fixed to the top after which the final gluing of the top to the legs can proceed.

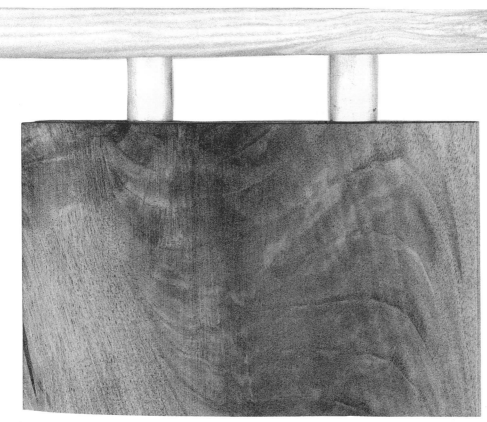

Leg detail

Take the trouble to do a dry run of this process to check that all the spacer spigots line up accurately and the shoulders seat properly on to the top edge of the legs. Deep-throated cramps are the best way to get direct pressure on to these joints, otherwise curved cramping bars and conventional sash cramps could be used, though this is both awkward and not very satisfactory. If you have a convenient beam or ceiling against which to work, you could consider using jacks or some form of go-bar to exert pressure in the right place. Improvisation can often be less costly than the 'correct' equipment, particularly if time is not a vital cost factor.

FINISHING

Finish will be determined mainly by the materials used, and the taste of the eventual owner. In this case the veneered panels were sprayed before final assembly with acid catalysed lacquer, and the walnut legs were oiled.

CUTTING LIST

Finished sizes

Top panel	1060 x 1060 x 19	MDF / Ply
Shelf panel	835 x 835 x 19	MDF / Ply

Lippings:

Top	4 x 1110 x 20 x 20	Ash
Shelf	4 x 855 x 10 x 10	Ash

Veneer for top and shelf panels; approximately 50 square feet including balancers (does not include waste)

Legs	4 x 330 x 220 x 35	Walnut
Spacers	4 x 70 x 20 diameter	Walnut/Ash

Copper tube (water tube : 22mm outside diameter, 1mm wall thickness)

OFFICE DESK
AND DRAWERS

I n this instance I wish to take a rather different approach and describe the thinking behind the design in more detail, and only offer a summary of the process of making. These are not exceptionally sophisticated structures by any means, but are unlikely to be successfully accomplished by an inexperienced maker.

As with most of the projects in this book, this desk, drawer unit and meeting table (see next chapter) were commissioned pieces. They were designed for a particular person with individual requirements, and for a particular room and space. Which is not to say that the ideas are exclusive to these items, both the practical and aesthetic requirements being familiar, nor that the furniture would only ever work in one specific place. It is, after all, a very rare interior that is designed with such rigid intensity that it cannot bear any intervention, and as most of us seem to suffer occasionally from a mysterious urge to move the furniture around, specific contextual and personal requirements are normally only the starting point in the history of a piece of furniture.

This commission arose as part of the refurbishment of a managing director's office, replacing a rather clumsy and worn reproduction partner's desk. The office building is early Georgian, the room in question modestly fitted out as a library. It is very much a working environment and while being nicely appointed is not intended as a show-piece interior. There is a notable absence of computer clutter and paper storage, these being handled elsewhere. The atmosphere approaches semi-domestic comfort, a feeling emphasised by French windows opening on to a carefully tended garden.

During the initial briefing, we established the desired position within the room for the main working surface, its ideal size and the way in which the customer used his existing desk. It soon became apparent that while a fair amount of paper passed through the office there was no need to provide a great deal of storage within the desk. This was especially significant in that it allowed greater flexibility in determining the visual weight of the design.

The conventional idea of an MD's desk is one of overtly expressed wealth and/or authority, calculated to impress, if not belittle, all who dare approach. This popular view is of course pure soap opera and, at its worst, is responsible for the most astonishing vulgarity. Thankfully not a whiff

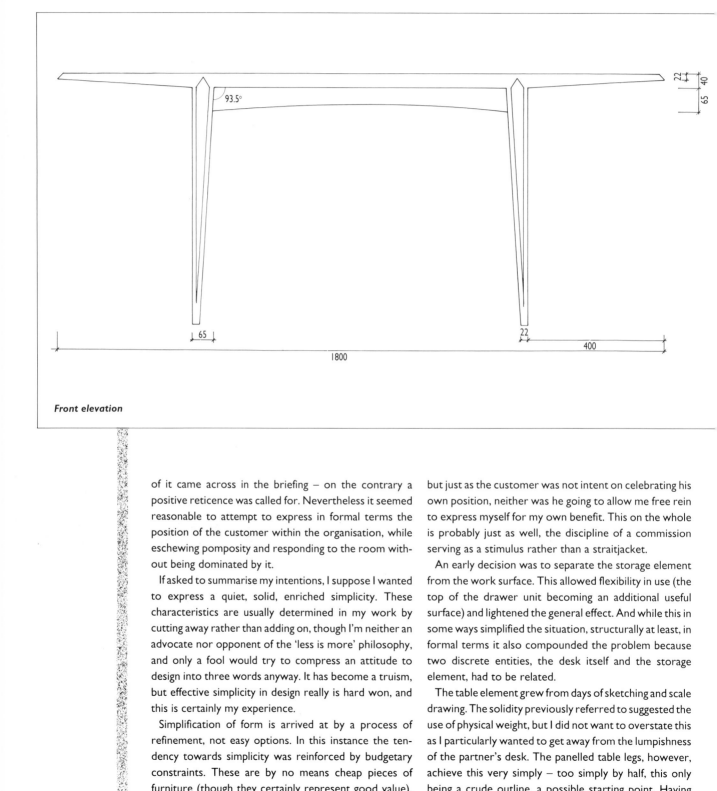

Front elevation

of it came across in the briefing – on the contrary a positive reticence was called for. Nevertheless it seemed reasonable to attempt to express in formal terms the position of the customer within the organisation, while eschewing pomposity and responding to the room without being dominated by it.

If asked to summarise my intentions, I suppose I wanted to express a quiet, solid, enriched simplicity. These characteristics are usually determined in my work by cutting away rather than adding on, though I'm neither an advocate nor opponent of the 'less is more' philosophy, and only a fool would try to compress an attitude to design into three words anyway. It has become a truism, but effective simplicity in design really is hard won, and this is certainly my experience.

Simplification of form is arrived at by a process of refinement, not easy options. In this instance the tendency towards simplicity was reinforced by budgetary constraints. These are by no means cheap pieces of furniture (though they certainly represent good value),

but just as the customer was not intent on celebrating his own position, neither was he going to allow me free rein to express myself for my own benefit. This on the whole is probably just as well, the discipline of a commission serving as a stimulus rather than a straitjacket.

An early decision was to separate the storage element from the work surface. This allowed flexibility in use (the top of the drawer unit becoming an additional useful surface) and lightened the general effect. And while this in some ways simplified the situation, structurally at least, in formal terms it also compounded the problem because two discrete entities, the desk itself and the storage element, had to be related.

The table element grew from days of sketching and scale drawing. The solidity previously referred to suggested the use of physical weight, but I did not want to overstate this as I particularly wanted to get away from the lumpishness of the partner's desk. The panelled table legs, however, achieve this very simply – too simply by half, this only being a crude outline, a possible starting point. Having

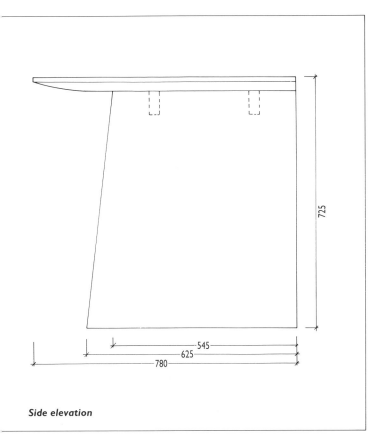

Side elevation

725

545
625
780

settled on this basic structural arrangement as an avenue to explore, the aim was then to endow the three planes with incident, detail, movement, interest. A number of scale elevation drawings were made to determine position and proportion. I find this important as it can be quite easy to fool yourself with optimistic sketching. (This in no way diminishes the importance of being able to draw freehand, it being a useful adjunct to, not a replacement of, that ability.)

It was at about this point that I began to see the desk as a solid wood piece. This was partly because the leg structure is ideal for holding a solid top, but mainly because solid wood affords opportunities for shaping and cutting into the material that are difficult to achieve with veneered surfaces. (Indeed it could be said that with veneer one is concerned solely with surface, while solid allows handling in the round. This is rather simplistic, but contains some truth.) Thus I began trying changes of section, and shaping edges and ends, to lift the composition by linear means. The thickness of the panels (all out

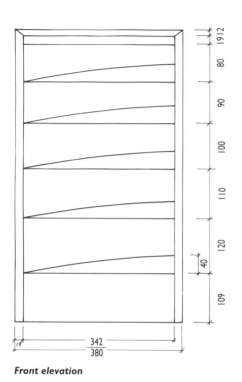

Front elevation

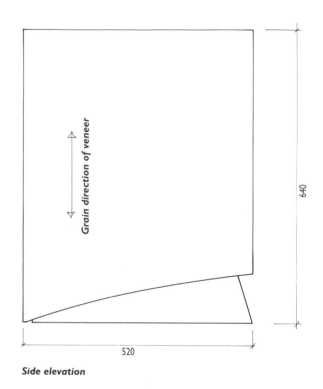

Grain direction of veneer

Side elevation

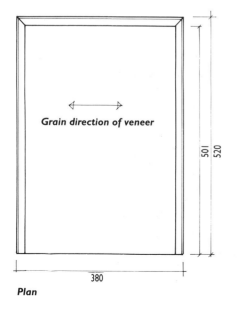

Grain direction of veneer

Plan

of 50mm and 75mm thick sections) was offset by tapering the legs and underside of the top towards the ends, the latter detail producing an illusion of lift, as does the underside of the oversailing front edge of the top, softened by a shallow curve as it noses forward.

The front edges of the legs lean back, leading the eye in and reducing their monolithic quality, and the double taper produces a curious effect in perspective. Rigorous symmetry was not a requirement here and the back of the desk (the user's side) was detailed differently to take advantage of this, as can be seen in the illustration. The horizontal edge was angled, resulting in a slight sense of forward movement, the legs emphatically carved with a diminishing V-groove.

Making this neat list is somewhat misleading as it does not express adequately the generally rather messy evolutionary process of development. Nor are the intellectual intentions the main point, these often being tacked on to the intuitive ideas as a kind of reinforcement, rather than a foundation.

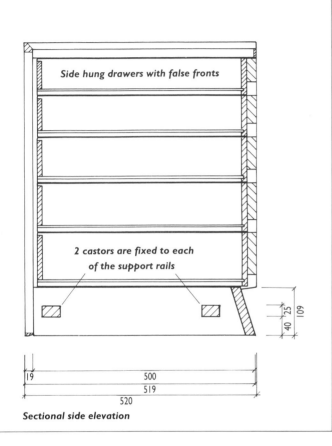

Side hung drawers with false fronts

2 castors are fixed to each
of the support rails

Sectional side elevation

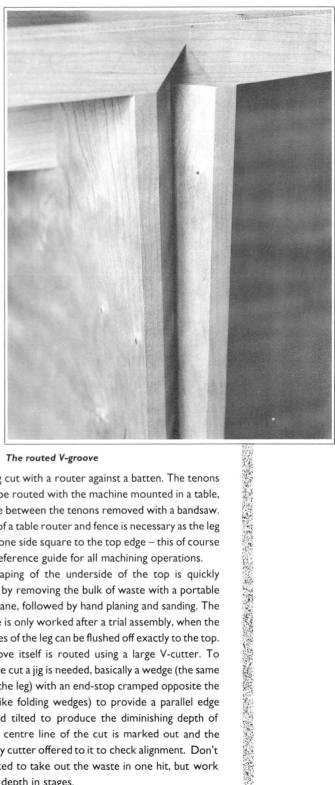

The routed V-groove

I shall only offer a very cursory account of the making processes, there being hardly any unfamiliar techniques to describe. The preparation of the leg taper is aided by the use of a thicknessing jig – basically a wedge with a stop, wide enough to take the boards prior to edge jointing. When sawing the bulk of the waste to produce the taper, remember that some timbers are very liable to cup and bow as the material is removed from one face. It is as well to make a generous allowance to compensate for this tendency, and to leave the sawn sections for a day or two before finishing to the final dimensions.

THE DESK

Having prepared and jointed the top and legs, the cross rails were tenoned into the legs. These rails provide some extra stiffness to the top which is hardly needed, but also brace the structure and help keep the legs square when they are assembled to the top. The legs are housed and stub tenoned to the top, the mortices and housing in the

top being cut with a router against a batten. The tenons can also be routed with the machine mounted in a table, the waste between the tenons removed with a bandsaw. The use of a table router and fence is necessary as the leg has only one side square to the top edge – this of course is your reference guide for all machining operations.

The shaping of the underside of the top is quickly achieved by removing the bulk of waste with a portable power plane, followed by hand planing and sanding. The V-groove is only worked after a trial assembly, when the back edges of the leg can be flushed off exactly to the top. The groove itself is routed using a large V-cutter. To centre the cut a jig is needed, basically a wedge (the same taper as the leg) with an end-stop cramped opposite the leg (i.e. like folding wedges) to provide a parallel edge guide, and tilted to produce the diminishing depth of cut. The centre line of the cut is marked out and the stationary cutter offered to it to check alignment. Don't be tempted to take out the waste in one hit, but work down to depth in stages.

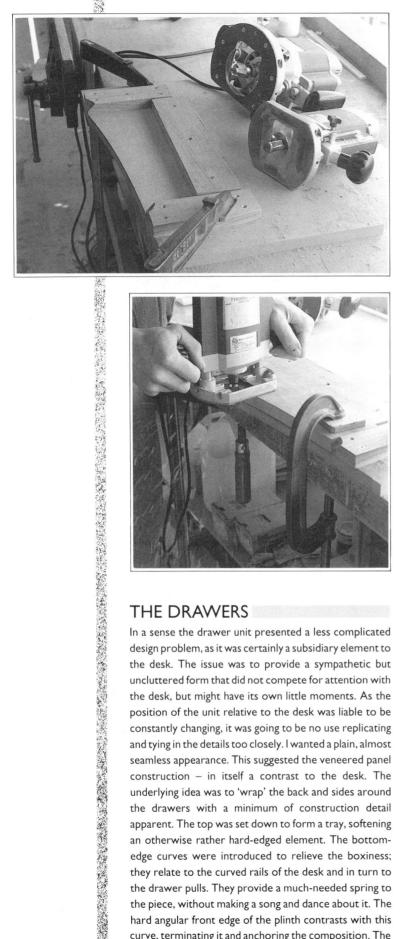

THE DRAWERS

In a sense the drawer unit presented a less complicated design problem, as it was certainly a subsidiary element to the desk. The issue was to provide a sympathetic but uncluttered form that did not compete for attention with the desk, but might have its own little moments. As the position of the unit relative to the desk was liable to be constantly changing, it was going to be no use replicating and tying in the details too closely. I wanted a plain, almost seamless appearance. This suggested the veneered panel construction – in itself a contrast to the desk. The underlying idea was to 'wrap' the back and sides around the drawers with a minimum of construction detail apparent. The top was set down to form a tray, softening an otherwise rather hard-edged element. The bottom-edge curves were introduced to relieve the boxiness; they relate to the curved rails of the desk and in turn to the drawer pulls. They provide a much-needed spring to the piece, without making a song and dance about it. The hard angular front edge of the plinth contrasts with this curve, terminating it and anchoring the composition. The

drawer pulls followed on, as it were, from the curve on the carcase. I now find them a mite too aggressive and verging on being laboured, something which can very easily result from the application of a successful detail to a different context. However, they work sufficiently well both from my own point of view and the customer's for them not to be dismissed completely. This is an instance where the made object tells a different story to the drawings, and is one of the chief risks – and joys – of any designer.

The construction consists of a veneered MDF carcase mitred and biscuited at the back edges, the top panel also biscuited in. Cramping up long mitres is at best a fraught business, particularly when dealing with veneered panels. We have found that screwing appropriately sized triangular sections of timber to hardboard and then cramping these to the veneered panels to provide angle blocks has been very effective. Time invested in making the blocks is more than made up for in accuracy and the reduction of subsequent cleaning up. (One tip: if you do use this method, keep the smooth side of the hardboard to the veneer – the textured side can make, as they say, a bad impression.)

To stiffen the carcase at the base, the plinth is set inside the carcase and biscuited. The plinth itself is solid maple mitred at the front and stiffened by tenoned cross rails.

Plinth detail

These rails are positioned according to the height of the castors and should allow the unit to clear the floor by at least 10mm to accommodate carpet pile. The drawers are all traditionally dovetailed, with mahogany sides, cherry fronts and pulls, and are side hung on maple runners, housed and screwed to the carcase.

Both the desk and storage were finished with teak oil, five coats being applied over approximately two weeks. When dry, they were cut back with 0000 wire wool and then burnished with dry polishing cloth.

Drawers being fitted

CUTTING LIST

Finished sizes
Office desk:

Top	1 x 1800 x 780 x 40	Cherry
Legs	2 x 715 x 625 x 65	Cherry
Rails	2 x 930 x 65 x 30	Maple

Mobile storage:
Carcase

Back	1 x 640 x 380 x 19	Veneered MDF
Sides	2 x 640 x 515 x 19	Veneered MDF
Top	1 x 342 x 501 x 19	Veneered MDF
Lippings	1500 x 19 x 15	Cherry
	5500 x 19 x 4	Cherry

Plinth

Sides	2 x 520 x 109 x 19	Maple
Front	1 x 342 x 125* x 19	Maple
	*extra width to accommodate bevels.	
Rails	2 x 372 x 40 x 25	Maple

Drawers

Fronts:	1 x 342 x 80 x 13	Cherry
	1 x 342 x 90 x 13	Cherry
	1 x 342 x 100 x 13	Cherry
	1 x 342 x 110 x 13	Cherry
	1 x 342 x 120 x 13	Cherry
False fronts/		
panels	5 x 342 x (widths as above) x 20	Cherry
Sides	10 x 470 x (widths as above) x 13	Mahogany
Backs	5 x 342 x (widths as above) x 13	Mahogany
Runners	10 x 420 x 19 x 6	Maple

4 x 40mm diameter twin wheel castors, square plate mounting.

OFFICE
MEETING TABLE

corners in order to stretch the length of composition as far as possible to compensate for its relatively small size and maximise its visual presence.

The top is conceived as an almost independent structure, essentially an inverted tray which fits precisely over the underframe. As far as is possible with timber, I wished the top to appear to be a completely homogeneous piece of material with no end grain or exposed lippings. To achieve this effect the two long sides were mitred to the top panel itself. The angled ends were constructed using laminated MDF (for the necessary thickness) to make the wedge section, which was butted and biscuited inside the two side rails. The top and side panels were prepared to exact size and lipped all round prior to veneering. Though these thin lippings are not seen on the mitred edge, they are an insurance against the inevitable wear that the edge will have to cope with. When preparing the veneer, sufficient length was left from the top panel to eventually apply to the ends, the grain following through as closely as possible. The wedge section end rails can be built up using any convenient thicknesses of MDF – it's hardly worth going to the expense of buying a sheet of 30mm just for two short rails (to say nothing of the need for an osteopath after attempting to lift it) – and then sawn and planed to the angle. The side rails are shaped using a bandsaw, then cleaned up accurately with a router

With the desk and drawer unit installed to the customer's satisfaction, some discussion followed as to the possibility of a secondary table to complement them. There were two basic functional requirements; to extend the surface area of the original desk to take paperwork awaiting processing – a glorified in-tray really – and to provide for the occasional informal meeting. Space was severely restricted, limiting the size of the piece, and as its position in the room would change quite frequently according to use, it had to be light enough to be moved easily. The space-saving flexibility of a drop leaf or extending table was rejected in favour of a modestly sized rigid design.

In developing this design, the original desk and drawers were used only as a starting point. To slavishly recycle the visual and constructional detailing at a smaller scale would not only have failed to succeed proportionally, as early sketching quickly revealed, but would have amounted to a lost opportunity. In jobs of this kind it is surely more stimulating to create a new, related concept, one that is capable of some autonomy. than simply to match an original. So I began by taking some of the more obvious visual details from the desk – the tapering legs, the angled edges, the curve of the rails and plinth – and began rearranging these in a way appropriate for a more lightweight construction.

One early and important decision was to use a veneered panel top, which of course affords a very different range of structural possibilities to the solid wood used in the desk. This was partly to reduce weight while achieving an apparently massive, thick top. The legs were placed at the

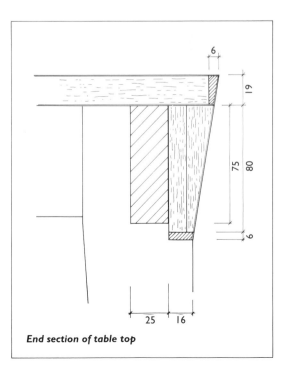

End section of table top

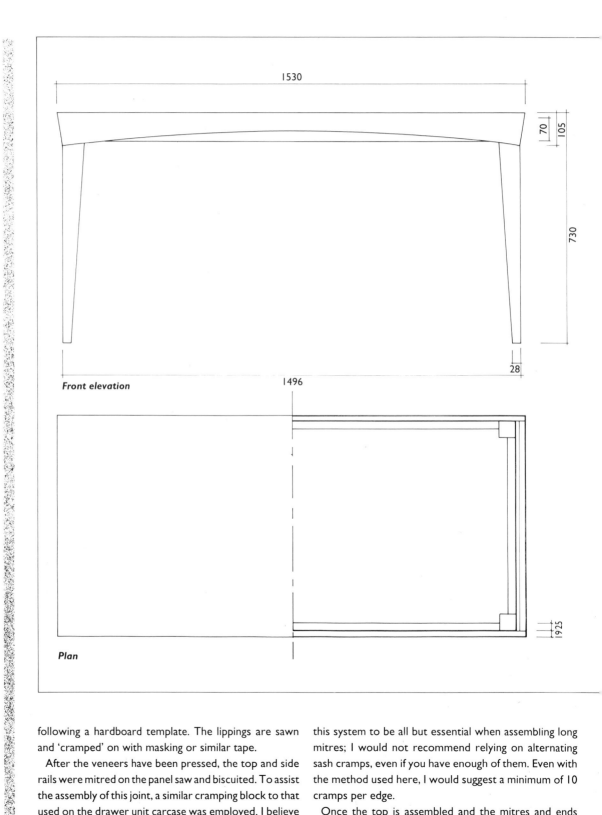

1530

70
105

730

28

Front elevation

1496

Plan

1925

following a hardboard template. The lippings are sawn and 'cramped' on with masking or similar tape.

After the veneers have been pressed, the top and side rails were mitred on the panel saw and biscuited. To assist the assembly of this joint, a similar cramping block to that used on the drawer unit carcase was employed. I believe this system to be all but essential when assembling long mitres; I would not recommend relying on alternating sash cramps, even if you have enough of them. Even with the method used here, I would suggest a minimum of 10 cramps per edge.

Once the top is assembled and the mitres and ends

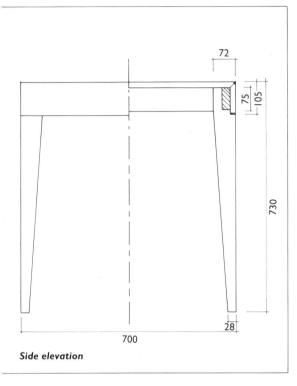

72

75 105

730

28

700

Side elevation

CUTTING LIST

Finished sizes

Rails	2 x 1400 x 70 x 25	Maple
	2 x 620 x 75 x 25	Maple
Legs	4 x 711 x 72 x 72	Cherry
Lippings	2 x 1530 x 20 x 6	Cherry
	2 x 700 x 20 x 6	Cherry
	2 x 662 x 20 x 6	Cherry
	4 x 105 x 20 x 6	Cherry
	2 x 1550 x 20 x 3	Cherry
	1 x 1518 x 688 x 18	MDF
	2 x 1518 x 97 x 18 (shaped)	MDF
	2 x 662 x 80 x 18	MDF
	2 x 662 x 80 x 12	MDF

Cherry veneer and backing veneer

carefully cleaned up, the ends are veneered. The veneer is taped in place to assist the alignment of the grain as closely as possible with that of the top panel and can be pressed using a prepared block and G cramps or simply ironed on, provided a UF resin glue is used, *not* PVA. If ironing on, use aluminium foil to protect the veneer from scorching and try one or two practice pieces to get the balance of speed and pressure right. (Of course, you can always use scotch glue, if, as they say, you have the technology.)

The legs are square tapered from 75mm below their top edge to the foot, allowing a square shoulder to be used on all the underframing rails. Before the taper or the mortise and tenons are cut, the top of the leg has to be notched out to fit inside the corner of the top tray – see illustration. The end faces of the leg have a section with a square shoulder removed to a depth of 16mm. The leg can then be offered up inside the top tray and the curved shoulder on the other outside face scribed off; this slightly curved shoulder can be sawn very close, then pared to fit the top exactly. The rails – in this case maple, to contrast with the cherry legs and top – were haunched tenoned into the legs. It is essential that the dimensions of the underframe

precisely match those of the inside of the top panel, so before cutting the tenons, double-check the shoulder length of the rails. The top panel should be a push fit on to the underframe, and the two are finally screwed together from the inside of the rails.

The finish will depend very much on the materials used. In this case, in order to match the finish of the desk, the table was oiled using teak oil. This took five or six coats over a period of about ten days, with gentle denibbing with fine wire wool between each coat.

The basic idea behind this design is capable of an enormous variety of interpretations. Great elaboration is possible, particularly in the treatment of the veneers and in the way the edges of the top reveal the underframe structure. If veneering is an impossibility, the MDF top is ideal for paint treatment, either sprayed or hand applied – and there's no shortage of books about that subject. This would also make the mitred construction unnecessary.

Alternatively there are hundreds, if not thousands, of plastic laminates that are cheap, hard wearing and requiring no specialist equipment for their use. And then there's leather, gilding...

Rod Wales was born in Zaire in 1950. Partly educated at Alleyn's School, Dulwich, he intended to study Art History, but five years on the periphery of the rock music business led in 1975 to the gates of Rycotewood. This was followed by a time at Buckinghamshire College as a furniture technician prior to attending the School for Craftsmen in Wood at Parnham from 1978 to 1980. On graduation he spent a five month period as assistant to Martin Grierson before setting up a workshop in Sussex in 1981. He was selected for the Crafts Council Index in 1986.